THE TREE OF LIFE

A Biblical Journey from Genesis to Revelation

Dr. Maxwell Shimba

Printed by Shimba Publishing LLC
Printed in the United States of America

TABLE OF CONTENTS

INTRODUCTION

The Tree of Life in Biblical Context

The Tree of Life, a recurring motif in the Bible, carries profound symbolic significance and theological depth. This enigmatic symbol appears throughout Scripture, weaving a narrative of divine provision, eternal life, and spiritual nourishment. Understanding its role across both the Old and New Testaments offers insight into its profound significance for God's people.

Defining the Tree of Life

The Tree of Life first emerges in the Garden of Eden, a lush paradise where it symbolizes God's provision and the promise of eternal life. In Genesis 2:9, the Tree of Life is described as being in the midst of the garden, alongside the Tree of Knowledge of Good and Evil. This dual presence represents the divine dichotomy of life and knowledge, obedience and disobedience. The Tree of Life is not merely a botanical entity but a symbol of the divine life and vitality that God bestows upon His creation.

In Genesis 3:22-24, the Tree of Life's significance is highlighted by its association with eternal life. After Adam and Eve's disobedience and their subsequent expulsion from Eden, the Tree of Life is guarded by cherubim, preventing humanity from accessing its life-sustaining fruit. This act serves as a poignant reminder of the consequences of sin and the separation it creates between humanity and the divine source of life.

The Tree of Life in the Wisdom Literature

The concept of the Tree of Life extends beyond Genesis into the Wisdom Books of the Bible. Proverbs, for instance, employs the Tree of Life metaphorically to represent wisdom, righteousness, and hope. In Proverbs 3:18, wisdom is likened to a Tree of Life, suggesting that those who embrace wisdom will experience a flourishing life. Similarly, Proverbs 11:30 and 13:12 associate the Tree of Life with the fruits of righteousness and hope, respectively, reinforcing its role as a symbol of spiritual well-being and fulfillment.

The Tree of Life in the Prophetic Books

The prophetic literature further develops the imagery of the Tree of Life. Ezekiel's vision in Ezekiel 47:12 describes a river flowing from the temple, with trees on its banks bearing fruit every month and leaves for healing. This vision illustrates the Tree of Life as a source of healing and restoration, symbolizing God's promise of renewal and abundance in the future kingdom.

Joel 2:22 and Isaiah 55:12 also reflect the Tree of Life's themes of restoration and joy. Joel speaks of the restoration of nature, while Isaiah envisions a transformed world where creation rejoices. These passages contribute to a broader understanding of the Tree of Life as integral to God's redemptive plan for His creation.

The Tree of Life in the New Testament

In the New Testament, the Tree of Life reappears in Revelation, providing a culmination of its biblical symbolism. Revelation 2:7 promises that those who overcome will eat from the Tree of Life in paradise, a clear reference to the eternal life and divine communion that God promises to His faithful. Revelation 22:2 further elaborates on this promise, depicting the Tree of Life in the new Jerusalem, with its leaves serving as a means of healing for the nations. Revelation 22:14

reiterates the Tree of Life's role in granting access to eternal life for those who follow God's commandments.

Theological Implications

The Tree of Life represents more than a physical tree; it is a profound symbol of divine life, wisdom, and restoration. Its presence in the Bible underscores God's intention to offer eternal life and spiritual nourishment to humanity. The Tree of Life embodies the ultimate goal of redemption and the fulfillment of God's promises to His people.

By tracing the Tree of Life from its origins in Eden to its final depiction in the new Jerusalem, this book aims to explore the depth of its significance and its role in the broader narrative of Scripture. Through this journey, readers will gain a richer understanding of God's eternal provision and the profound spiritual truths embedded in this powerful biblical symbol.

The Aim and Theological Implications of Tracing the Tree of Life from Genesis to Revelation

The Tree of Life is a profound symbol that threads its way through the entirety of Scripture, from Genesis to Revelation. This biblical motif, first encountered in the Garden of Eden and culminating in the new Jerusalem, represents a deep and abiding aspect of God's relationship with humanity. The purpose of tracing the Tree of Life through the Bible is to uncover its evolving significance and understand its theological implications for the faithful.

Purpose of Tracing the Tree of Life

The aim of tracing the Tree of Life from Genesis to Revelation is multifaceted. First, it allows for a comprehensive examination of its symbolic role throughout the biblical narrative. By exploring the Tree of Life in its various contexts—beginning in the Edenic paradise, through the wisdom literature, the prophetic visions, and the apocalyptic promises—one can appreciate how its symbolism develops and deepens over time.

1. Uncovering Symbolic Evolution: The Tree of Life initially appears as a literal and physical entity in Genesis, representing divine provision and eternal life. As Scripture progresses, its symbolism expands to encompass broader themes such as wisdom, righteousness, healing, and eternal life. Tracing this evolution reveals how the Tree of Life's symbolism adapts to different contexts while retaining its core significance.

2. Theological Understanding: By examining the Tree of Life through the biblical narrative, we gain insight into its theological implications. Each mention of the Tree of Life

offers a unique perspective on divine promises, human responses, and the ultimate goal of salvation. Understanding its role in various parts of Scripture helps to construct a cohesive theological framework that highlights its importance in God's plan for creation and redemption.

3. Connecting Old and New Testaments: The Tree of Life serves as a bridge between the Old and New Testaments, linking the early promises made in Eden with their fulfillment in the eschatological vision of Revelation. Tracing this motif across both testaments illustrates the continuity of God's redemptive plan and the consistency of His promises from the beginning of creation to the end of time.

Theological Implications

1. Divine Provision and Eternal Life: In Genesis, the Tree of Life symbolizes God's provision of eternal life and the fullness of divine blessings. Its removal from humanity after the fall signifies the separation caused by sin and the need for redemption. The promise of reaccess to the Tree of Life in Revelation underscores the restoration of what was lost and the ultimate fulfillment of God's promise of eternal life.

2. Wisdom and Righteousness: In the wisdom literature, the Tree of Life metaphorically represents wisdom

and righteousness. Proverbs associates it with the fruits of living a life in alignment with God's will, illustrating how divine wisdom leads to spiritual and moral vitality. This perspective enriches our understanding of how living in accordance with divine principles aligns with the Tree of Life's symbolism.

3. Healing and Restoration: The prophetic literature introduces the Tree of Life as a symbol of healing and restoration. Ezekiel's vision and the imagery in Revelation emphasize the Tree of Life's role in restoring creation and providing spiritual healing. This aspect highlights the transformative power of divine intervention in restoring a fallen world.

4. Eschatological Fulfillment: Revelation's depiction of the Tree of Life in the new Jerusalem brings the biblical narrative to its climactic conclusion. It represents the ultimate fulfillment of God's promises and the realization of an eternal state where divine life and blessing are fully restored to humanity. This eschatological vision provides hope and assurance of the final and complete restoration of creation.

Tracing the Tree of Life from Genesis to Revelation offers a deep and enriching exploration of one of the Bible's most significant symbols. It reveals how the Tree of Life encapsulates themes of divine provision, eternal life, wisdom, righteousness, healing, and eschatological fulfillment. Understanding these theological implications enriches our grasp of God's redemptive plan and the profound ways in which He interacts with creation throughout the entirety of Scripture.

This journey through the Tree of Life not only illuminates its symbolic depth but also connects the rich tapestry of biblical themes, offering a holistic view of God's enduring promise and His ultimate purpose for humanity.

DR. MAXWELL SHIMBA

THE TREE OF LIFE IN GENESIS

Genesis 2:9: Introduction in the Garden of Eden

Genesis 2:9 stands as a pivotal moment in the biblical narrative, introducing the Tree of Life into the Garden of Eden. This verse provides essential insights into the nature of the Tree of Life and its profound significance within the creation story. To fully appreciate its impact, it is crucial to understand the context in which this tree is introduced and its implications for humanity.

Contextual Background

The Garden of Eden, described in Genesis 2, is a pristine and lush environment created by God as a dwelling place for humanity. This garden is portrayed as a paradise of divine provision, where every plant and tree serves a specific purpose. Within this verdant expanse, the Tree of Life and the Tree of Knowledge of Good and Evil are mentioned, setting the stage for their critical roles in the narrative.

Genesis 2:9 reads: "And out of the ground made the Lord God to grow every tree that is pleasant to the sight, and good for food; the tree of life also in the midst of the garden, and the tree of knowledge of good and evil." This verse highlights two key aspects: the nature of the Tree of Life and its placement within the Garden.

The Nature of the Tree of Life

1. Symbolism of the Tree of Life: The Tree of Life is more than a physical tree; it symbolizes divine provision and eternal vitality. Its presence in the Garden of Eden represents God's intention to offer life and sustenance to humanity. Unlike the other trees that are described as "pleasant to the sight, and good for food," the Tree of Life embodies a deeper, spiritual dimension of life that is intimately connected with the divine.

2. Eternal Life: The Tree of Life is associated with eternal life. In the context of the Garden, it signifies the ongoing and unending life that God intended for humanity. By partaking of its fruit, Adam and Eve would have experienced continuous divine nourishment and eternal

existence. The tree, therefore, serves as a tangible symbol of the divine gift of eternal life, a life uninterrupted by death or decay.

The Placement of the Tree of Life

1. Central Location: The Tree of Life is described as being "in the midst of the garden," indicating its central importance in the divine plan for creation. Its central location underscores its significance as the source of life and sustenance, integral to the well-being of humanity. This placement also emphasizes that access to the Tree of Life was meant to be a fundamental aspect of human existence in the Garden.

2. Contrast with the Tree of Knowledge of Good and Evil: Genesis 2:9 introduces the Tree of Life alongside the Tree of Knowledge of Good and Evil. The juxtaposition of these two trees highlights a critical choice for humanity. While the Tree of Life represents divine provision and eternal life, the Tree of Knowledge represents the possibility of human choice and moral discernment. The presence of both trees in the Garden creates a dynamic of choice that is central to the narrative of human freedom and responsibility.

Theological Implications

1. Divine Provision and Human Relationship: The Tree of Life symbolizes the abundant provision and intimate relationship that God intended for humanity. Its presence in the Garden represents God's desire for a close, sustaining relationship with His creation. By offering the Tree of Life, God provides a means for humanity to experience and enjoy the fullness of life as He designed it.

2. Human Freedom and Responsibility: The introduction of the Tree of Knowledge of Good and Evil alongside the Tree of Life introduces the concept of human freedom and moral choice. The choice to obey or disobey God, represented by the trees, is a central theme in the narrative. The presence of the Tree of Life emphasizes the possibility of eternal life through obedience and faithfulness to God.

3. The Fall and Its Consequences: The subsequent fall of humanity and the expulsion from Eden underscore the significance of the Tree of Life. After Adam and Eve's disobedience, access to the Tree of Life is barred, symbolizing the separation from divine life caused by sin. The loss of access to the Tree of Life illustrates the profound impact of sin on the relationship between humanity and God, and sets

the stage for the redemptive themes that will unfold throughout Scripture.

Genesis 2:9 introduces the Tree of Life as a symbol of divine provision and eternal life, central to the Garden of Eden and the creation narrative. Its presence in the Garden represents God's intention for humanity to live in close communion with Him, enjoying the fullness of life He offers. The contrast with the Tree of Knowledge of Good and Evil introduces the theme of human choice, setting the stage for the unfolding story of humanity's relationship with God. Understanding the significance of the Tree of Life in this context enriches our grasp of the biblical narrative and its theological implications for the rest of Scripture.

Genesis 3:22-24: The Tree of Life and the Expulsion from Eden

Genesis 3:22-24 marks a significant turning point in the biblical narrative, detailing the aftermath of humanity's disobedience and the subsequent expulsion from the Garden of Eden. This passage not only highlights the consequences of Adam and Eve's sin but also emphasizes the role of the Tree of Life in the broader context of divine justice and redemption. Understanding these verses provides insight into the theological implications of the Tree of Life and its symbolic significance within the story of the fall.

The Passage: Genesis 3:22-24

The passage reads:

"22 Then the Lord God said, 'Behold, the man has become like one of Us, to know good and evil; and now, lest he put out his hand and take also of the tree of life, and eat, and live forever—' 23 therefore the Lord God sent him out of the garden of Eden to till the ground from which he was taken. 24 So He drove out the man; and He placed cherubim at the east of the garden of Eden, and a flaming sword which turned every way, to guard the way to the tree of life."

Theological Implications

1. Human Transformation and Divine Concern:

- Knowledge of Good and Evil: The phrase "the man has become like one of Us, to know good and evil" reflects a pivotal change in humanity's condition. The knowledge of good and evil represents a profound shift from innocence to moral awareness, resulting from Adam and Eve's disobedience. This newfound awareness brought both the potential for deeper understanding and the capacity for sin.

- Divine Concern: The Lord's concern that Adam and Eve might "take also of the tree of life, and eat, and live forever" underscores the gravity of their situation. The Tree of Life, once a symbol of divine provision and eternal vitality, could not be accessed by sinful humanity. The implication is that allowing them to eat from it would result in an eternal state of separation from God, marked by sin and corruption. Thus, the divine decision to prevent access to the Tree of Life was an act of mercy designed to protect humanity from an eternity of suffering.

2. Expulsion from Eden:

- Purpose of the Expulsion: The expulsion from Eden served several purposes. It was both a consequence of sin and a preventive measure. By sending Adam and Eve out of the Garden, God implemented a necessary separation between sin and the eternal life symbolized by the Tree of Life. This separation ensured that humanity could no longer access the tree and thereby live forever in a fallen state.

- Labor and Mortality: The command to "till the ground from which he was taken" indicates a shift from a life of ease in Eden to one of labor and struggle. This change reflects the broader consequences of sin, including the introduction of toil and mortality. The ground, which was once a source of effortless provision, now becomes a place of hard work and struggle.

3. Guarding the Tree of Life:

- Cherubim and the Flaming Sword: The placement of cherubim and a flaming sword to guard the entrance to the Garden represents a powerful symbol of divine protection and the severance of access to eternal life. Cherubim are often associated with the divine presence and protection, and the flaming sword that "turned every way" underscores the impenetrable barrier now separating humanity from the Tree of Life.

- Symbolism of the Barrier: The barrier not only protects the Tree of Life but also serves as a reminder of the separation caused by sin. It symbolizes the need for redemption and the eventual restoration of access to eternal life through divine intervention. The image of the guarded Tree of Life reflects the seriousness of sin and the need for a mediator to restore the broken relationship between God and humanity.

Theological Reflections

1. The Nature of Sin and Its Consequences:

- Separation from God: The expulsion from Eden illustrates the profound impact of sin on the relationship between humanity and God. Sin introduces a barrier that separates humanity from divine life and blessings. The Tree of Life, once accessible and a symbol of divine favor, becomes inaccessible due to the consequences of disobedience.

- Need for Redemption: The guarded Tree of Life foreshadows the need for redemption and restoration. Throughout Scripture, the promise of redemption and the eventual reaccess to eternal life are central themes. The barrier around the Tree of Life highlights the necessity of a savior who would bridge the gap caused by sin and restore humanity's relationship with God.

2. Eschatological Implications:

- Restoration in Revelation: The concept of the Tree of Life is revisited in Revelation 22:2, where it reappears in the new Jerusalem, providing healing and eternal nourishment. The restoration of access to the Tree of Life signifies the ultimate fulfillment of God's redemptive plan and the complete restoration of the divine relationship with humanity.

- Fulfillment of Promise: The expulsion from Eden and the guarding of the Tree of Life mark the beginning of a narrative that culminates in the eschatological vision of Revelation. The eventual reaccess to the Tree of Life symbolizes the final victory over sin and death, and the realization of God's promise of eternal life for those who overcome.

Genesis 3:22-24 captures a critical moment in the biblical story, highlighting the consequences of humanity's sin and the subsequent expulsion from Eden. The Tree of Life, once a symbol of divine provision and eternal life, becomes a guarded symbol of separation due to sin. This passage not only underscores the seriousness of disobedience but also points forward to the promise of restoration and redemption. Understanding this passage enriches our appreciation of the Tree of Life's role in the biblical narrative and its theological significance as we trace its symbolism from Genesis to Revelation.

Theological Implications: Understanding the Tree of Life as a Symbol of Eternal Life and Divine Provision

The Tree of Life is one of the most potent and enduring symbols in the Bible, representing eternal life and divine provision. From its first appearance in the Garden of Eden to its reemergence in the book of Revelation, the Tree of Life serves as a profound metaphor for God's intentions for humanity. In this chapter, we will explore the theological implications of the Tree of Life, focusing on its symbolism as both a source of eternal life and a representation of God's continual provision for His creation.

The Tree of Life as a Symbol of Eternal Life

1. Eternal Life in the Garden of Eden:

- Genesis 2:9: The Tree of Life is introduced in the Garden of Eden, representing the possibility of eternal life for Adam and Eve. It stands as a divine gift, symbolizing the life that comes directly from God, unending and full of vitality. The presence of the Tree of Life in Eden suggests that eternal life was part of God's original design for humanity, contingent upon their obedience and trust in Him.

- Genesis 3:22-24: After the fall, humanity's access to the Tree of Life is severed, signifying the loss of eternal life due to sin. The expulsion from Eden and the guarding of the Tree of Life with cherubim and a flaming sword emphasize the gravity of this loss. The Tree of Life becomes a symbol of what was forfeited—eternal life in communion with God.

2. The Promise of Eternal Life in Scripture:

- Proverbs and Wisdom Literature: The Tree of Life reappears metaphorically in the wisdom literature, particularly in Proverbs, where it symbolizes the life-giving power of wisdom, righteousness, and hope. Proverbs 3:18 describes wisdom as a Tree of Life to those who embrace it, suggesting that living according to divine wisdom is a path to life in its fullest sense, hinting at the restoration of what was lost in Eden.

- Revelation 22:2: The ultimate fulfillment of the Tree of Life's symbolism is found in the new Jerusalem, where it stands as a source of healing and eternal nourishment for the nations. The Tree of Life's presence in the eternal city signifies the restoration of eternal life to humanity, now purified and redeemed through God's plan of salvation. This eschatological vision confirms that eternal life, once lost, will be fully restored to those who are faithful.

3. Theological Reflection on Eternal Life:

- Eternal Life as God's Intent: The consistent presence of the Tree of Life throughout Scripture indicates that eternal life is not only a future hope but was God's original intent for humanity. The biblical narrative portrays eternal life as a central theme, intertwined with the concepts of divine fellowship, obedience, and redemption.

- The Role of Jesus Christ: In Christian theology, Jesus Christ is often seen as the fulfillment of the Tree of Life, offering eternal life to all who believe in Him. John 14:6 presents Jesus as "the way, the truth, and the life," embodying the eternal life that the Tree of Life symbolized. Through His life, death, and resurrection, Jesus restores the possibility of eternal life to humanity, bridging the gap created by sin.

The Tree of Life as a Symbol of Divine Provision

1. Provision in the Garden of Eden:

- Divine Generosity: The Garden of Eden, as described in Genesis, was a place of abundant provision, where every need of Adam and Eve was met. The Tree of Life, situated at the center of this garden, was the ultimate symbol of God's generosity and provision. It represented not only physical sustenance but also spiritual and eternal sustenance, embodying the fullness of life that God intended for humanity.

- Life Sustained by God: The Tree of Life's central location in the garden underscores the idea that life—true, abundant, and eternal life—comes only from God. The nourishment it provided was not merely physical but was a sign of the spiritual and eternal life that flows from a direct relationship with the Creator.

2. Ongoing Divine Provision:

- The Role of Divine Wisdom: In Proverbs, the Tree of Life is associated with wisdom, righteousness, and hope, indicating that God's provision extends beyond physical needs to include moral and spiritual guidance. Wisdom, in this sense, is a form of divine provision, enabling humanity to live in harmony with God's will and to experience life as He intended.

- Healing and Restoration: In Revelation, the Tree of Life provides leaves "for the healing of the nations" (Revelation 22:2). This imagery reinforces the concept of the Tree of Life as a source of divine provision, now extended to all of creation. The healing properties of the tree's leaves suggest that God's provision includes not only sustenance and life but also restoration and wholeness, addressing the brokenness caused by sin.

3. Theological Reflection on Divine Provision:

- God as the Source of All Life: The Tree of Life consistently points back to the truth that God is the ultimate source of life. Whether in the paradisiacal setting of Eden, in the wisdom of righteous living, or in the eschatological vision of the new Jerusalem, the Tree of Life symbolizes God's unwavering provision for His creation. This provision is not limited to physical needs but encompasses spiritual nourishment and the promise of eternal life.

- The Relationship Between Provision and Obedience: The access to the Tree of Life in Eden was contingent upon obedience to God's command. The loss of access due to sin illustrates the relationship between divine provision and human obedience. Throughout Scripture, God's provision is often tied to the covenant relationship He establishes with His people, where obedience and faithfulness are keys to receiving the fullness of His blessings.

The Tree of Life, as presented in the Bible, serves as a rich symbol of both eternal life and divine provision. It encapsulates God's original intent for humanity—a life of abundance, health, and eternal communion with Him. The loss of access to the Tree of Life due to sin underscores the tragic consequences of disobedience, yet it also sets the stage for the redemptive work of God, culminating in the promise of restored access in the new Jerusalem.

Understanding the Tree of Life in this light deepens our appreciation of God's grace and His desire for humanity to share in His eternal life. It also challenges us to live in a way that reflects our dependence on His provision and our longing for the eternal life that He offers through Jesus Christ. The Tree of Life, therefore, is not merely an ancient symbol but a living testament to the life-giving power and generosity of God, woven throughout the narrative of Scripture and central to the hope of the Christian faith.

CHAPTER 02

THE TREE OF LIFE IN THE WISDOM BOOKS

Proverbs 3:18: The Tree of Life as Wisdom and Understanding

In the Wisdom Books, particularly in Proverbs, the Tree of Life takes on a more metaphorical significance. While in Genesis, the Tree of Life was a literal tree providing eternal life, in Proverbs it becomes a symbol for wisdom, understanding, and righteousness. Proverbs 3:18 offers a profound connection between the Tree of Life and the pursuit of wisdom:

"She is a tree of life to those who take hold of her; those who hold her fast will be blessed." (Proverbs 3:18, NIV)

This verse speaks of wisdom (personified as a woman) as being akin to the Tree of Life. In this chapter, we will explore how Proverbs uses the imagery of the Tree of Life to convey deeper spiritual truths about the pursuit of wisdom and its life-giving properties.

The Symbolism of Wisdom as the Tree of Life

1. The Nature of Wisdom in Proverbs:

- Personification of Wisdom: In Proverbs, wisdom is often personified as a woman who calls out to humanity, offering guidance, insight, and the path to life. Proverbs 3:18 underscores this personification by describing wisdom as "a tree of life," implying that wisdom, like the Tree of Life, provides life-giving sustenance and eternal blessings to those who pursue it.

- A Source of Life: Just as the Tree of Life in Genesis represented God's provision for eternal life, wisdom in Proverbs is portrayed as something that provides spiritual and moral vitality. Those who "take hold" of wisdom and live by its principles experience life in its fullest sense—marked by flourishing, righteousness, and alignment with God's will. This life is not only about the physical or material realm but also encompasses spiritual growth and moral integrity.

2. Wisdom as a Path to Blessing:

- "She is a tree of life to those who take hold of her": This phrase suggests that wisdom is available to everyone, but its benefits are only realized by those who actively pursue and embrace it. Just as Adam and Eve were required to choose to eat from the Tree of Life, so too must individuals choose to seek and hold fast to wisdom. The act of "taking hold" indicates a conscious, deliberate effort to pursue a life aligned with God's truth.

- The Promise of Blessing: Those who "hold her fast" are promised blessings. This is a key theme in Proverbs: living a life grounded in wisdom leads to a life marked by peace, prosperity, and spiritual fulfillment. Wisdom provides the framework for navigating life's challenges in a way that is pleasing to God and beneficial to the individual, offering a form of life that mirrors the eternal life symbolized by the Tree of Life.

Wisdom and the Tree of Life: Theological Implications

1. Wisdom as a Reflection of Divine Life:

- Life in Harmony with God's Will: Wisdom in Proverbs is often seen as the key to living in harmony with

God's will. The Tree of Life represents eternal life, and in this context, wisdom offers a path to a life that reflects divine principles. By choosing wisdom, a person chooses life—both in the present sense of flourishing and in the ultimate sense of eternal life with God.

- Restoration of the Lost Tree of Life: The connection between wisdom and the Tree of Life suggests that wisdom plays a role in restoring what was lost in the Garden of Eden. While access to the literal Tree of Life was barred after the fall, wisdom offers a form of life that brings individuals closer to God and His eternal purposes. In this way, wisdom serves as a metaphorical "return" to the life that God originally intended for humanity.

2. Wisdom's Role in Personal and Communal Flourishing:

- Personal Transformation: Wisdom transforms individuals by guiding their thoughts, actions, and decisions in ways that align with God's truth. Like the Tree of Life, wisdom nourishes the soul, offering clarity and understanding that lead to a fruitful and prosperous life. This transformation is not just intellectual but also moral, as wisdom shapes a person's character to reflect righteousness.

- Communal Impact: While wisdom benefits individuals, it also has a broader impact on communities. A society built on wisdom and righteousness will experience peace, justice, and prosperity. Proverbs frequently emphasizes the communal benefits of wisdom, suggesting that a wise person contributes to the well-being of others. In this sense, wisdom, like the Tree of Life, offers sustenance not only to the individual but to the community as a whole.

Comparing the Tree of Life in Genesis and Proverbs

1. Physical vs. Metaphorical Life:

- In Genesis, the Tree of Life is a literal tree whose fruit provides eternal life, and its physical presence signifies God's divine provision. Eating from it would have ensured unending life in communion with God.

- In Proverbs, the Tree of Life takes on a metaphorical dimension, symbolizing the life-giving power of wisdom. While wisdom does not offer physical immortality, it provides a form of spiritual and moral life that reflects God's eternal nature. The person who pursues wisdom experiences a flourishing life, which, in its fullness, hints at the eternal life that God promises through His redemptive plan.

2. Choice and Access:

- In Genesis, access to the Tree of Life was dependent on Adam and Eve's obedience to God. After their disobedience, they were barred from the tree, highlighting the tragic loss of divine life due to sin.

- In Proverbs, wisdom is available to all who seek it. Access to the metaphorical Tree of Life, representing wisdom, is open to everyone, but it requires a conscious decision to embrace and hold fast to wisdom's principles. This reflects the biblical theme that the path to life is through obedience to God's word and the pursuit of righteousness.

Practical Implications for Believers Today

1. Pursuing Wisdom as the Path to Life:

- Proverbs 3:18 encourages believers to actively pursue wisdom as the key to a life that reflects God's goodness. In practical terms, this means seeking understanding through Scripture, prayer, and a life of integrity. Just as Adam and Eve were called to take from the Tree of Life, believers are called to take hold of wisdom, which offers spiritual nourishment and guidance in a complex world.

- Holding Fast to Wisdom: The imagery of "holding fast" to wisdom implies dedication and perseverance. In a world filled with competing voices and distractions, holding onto wisdom requires intentionality. This calls believers to focus on building a life grounded in God's truth, even when faced with challenges and temptations.

2. Wisdom's Role in Spiritual Growth:

- Embracing wisdom is a lifelong journey of spiritual growth. As believers take hold of wisdom, they experience the kind of life that God intends—one marked by peace, righteousness, and eternal significance. Just as the Tree of Life in Revelation offers healing to the nations, wisdom has the power to bring restoration and healing to the soul.

Proverbs 3:18 reveals that wisdom, like the Tree of Life, offers a path to flourishing, blessed living for those who take hold of it. The theological implications of this metaphor are profound, showing that wisdom provides spiritual sustenance, moral guidance, and access to the divine life that God intended for humanity. As the Tree of Life represented eternal life in Genesis, wisdom represents a form of life that mirrors this eternal nature by aligning individuals with God's will and purposes.

For believers today, pursuing wisdom is not just a matter of intellectual growth but a spiritual journey toward the abundant life that God offers. By holding fast to wisdom, we experience the blessing and sustenance that comes from living in harmony with God's truth, which ultimately leads us to the fullness of life both now and in eternity.

Proverbs 11:30: The Fruit of Righteousness as the Tree of Life

In the wisdom literature, especially in the book of Proverbs, the Tree of Life is used metaphorically to convey profound spiritual truths. Proverbs 11:30 provides an essential connection between righteousness and the Tree of Life:

"The fruit of the righteous is a tree of life, and the one who is wise saves lives." (Proverbs 11:30, NIV)

This verse portrays righteousness as producing fruit that brings life to others, likening it to the Tree of Life. It suggests that living righteously not only brings spiritual vitality to the individual but also nurtures and sustains the community. In this chapter, we will explore how the fruit of righteousness is compared to the Tree of Life, and the theological implications of this connection.

Righteousness and the Tree of Life

1. The Nature of Righteousness in Proverbs:

- Righteousness as Moral Integrity: In the book of Proverbs, righteousness is portrayed as a life of moral integrity, alignment with God's principles, and faithfulness to His commandments. It encompasses living justly, with compassion, and in harmony with God's law. Proverbs emphasizes that righteousness leads to flourishing, not only for the individual but for the entire community. This flourishing is likened to the life-giving power of the Tree of Life.

- Righteousness Bears Fruit: The phrase "the fruit of the righteous" suggests that righteousness is not a passive state but an active one that bears tangible results. Just as a tree produces fruit that provides nourishment and sustenance, the life of a righteous person produces outcomes that benefit others. The fruit of righteousness symbolizes the positive impact that living in alignment with God's will has on the individual and those around them.

2. The Fruit of Righteousness as a Tree of Life

- Life-Giving Power of Righteousness: Proverbs 11:30 connects the fruit of righteousness to the Tree of Life, suggesting that righteous living has the power to impart life.

Just as the Tree of Life in Genesis symbolized the divine source of eternal life, righteousness brings a form of spiritual vitality and blessing that sustains not only the individual but also those they influence. Righteous living, therefore, becomes a source of life, growth, and renewal, reflecting the eternal life that the Tree of Life symbolizes.

- The Impact of Righteous Living: The image of the fruit of the righteous being like a Tree of Life implies that those who live righteously create environments where others can thrive. Their actions, words, and choices produce "fruit" that nourishes those around them. This could be seen in the way a righteous person promotes justice, peace, and goodness in their community, offering a form of spiritual sustenance to those who encounter them.

The Theological Implications of Righteousness as a Tree of Life

1. Righteousness as a Source of Spiritual Nourishment:

- Reflecting God's Character: In Proverbs, righteousness is not merely a set of ethical behaviors but reflects the very character of God. Just as God is the source of all life, those who live righteously mirror God's life-giving nature. By living in accordance with divine wisdom and justice, the righteous person becomes a conduit of God's blessing and sustenance, offering life to others.

- Spiritual Nourishment for the Community: The fruit of the righteous as a Tree of Life implies that righteous living has a communal aspect. It is not limited to personal piety but extends to the flourishing of others. The righteous person's influence brings spiritual nourishment, guidance, and support to those around them. In this way, the fruit of righteousness helps to build a healthy, thriving community.

2. Restoration of What Was Lost:

- The Echo of Eden: The Tree of Life in Genesis represented access to eternal life and God's continual provision. After the fall, humanity lost direct access to the Tree of Life, symbolizing the severance from divine life due to sin. In Proverbs 11:30, righteousness is described as a new kind of Tree of Life, suggesting that righteous living offers a form of restored access to divine life. Though humanity cannot physically eat from the Tree of Life in Eden, the fruit of righteousness offers spiritual sustenance that reflects the life-giving power of that original tree.

\- Righteousness and Redemption: The association of righteousness with the Tree of Life points to the broader biblical theme of redemption. Righteousness, as described in Proverbs, offers a way to participate in God's ongoing work of renewal and restoration. Living righteously is part of God's plan for redeeming creation, and those who pursue righteousness bring a glimpse of the restored life that will be fully realized in the eschatological future, where the Tree of Life reappears in the new Jerusalem (Revelation 22:2).

3. Wisdom and the Saving of Lives:

\- "The One Who Is Wise Saves Lives": The latter part of Proverbs 11:30 ties wisdom and righteousness together, showing that those who live wisely and righteously not only experience life themselves but also help save others. The connection between wisdom and saving lives further emphasizes the communal and redemptive nature of righteousness. The righteous person, through their wisdom, acts in ways that lead others to life, both in practical and spiritual senses.

\- Evangelism and Spiritual Guidance: From a theological perspective, this verse can be seen as an early hint of the evangelical role that the righteous play in leading others to salvation. While Proverbs does not speak directly of the gospel, the idea that "the one who is wise saves lives" can be understood as an encouragement for the righteous to guide others toward the path of life, which ultimately points toward the fullness of life found in Christ.

Practical Implications for Believers Today

1. Living a Life That Bears Fruit:

- Pursuing Righteousness: Proverbs 11:30 challenges believers to live righteously, not only for their personal benefit but for the sake of others. The image of the fruit of the righteous as a Tree of Life invites us to consider how our actions, decisions, and relationships produce life-giving results. Are we living in a way that nourishes and supports those around us, or are we focused solely on ourselves? The fruit of righteousness is meant to be shared, benefiting the broader community.

- Cultivating Wisdom and Saving Lives: The call to "save lives" through wisdom highlights the responsibility of believers to influence others positively. Whether this means providing guidance, offering compassion, or leading others toward a deeper relationship with God, the wisdom and righteousness we cultivate should have an outward, life-saving impact.

2. Righteousness as a Path to Spiritual Vitality:

- Spiritual Growth: Righteous living leads to spiritual growth and vitality. Like the Tree of Life, which provides sustenance and eternal life, righteousness nourishes the soul and brings us closer to God. The more we align our lives with God's principles, the more we experience the fullness of life that He offers. This spiritual vitality is not only for ourselves but overflows to others, inviting them to partake in the life we've found in God.

- Being a Blessing to Others: The fruit of righteousness is intended to be a blessing to others. Just as a tree bears fruit for others to eat, our righteous living should produce fruit that benefits those around us. This may take the form of kindness, generosity, justice, or encouragement—actions that bring life, hope, and sustenance to a world in need of God's presence.

Proverbs 11:30 presents the powerful image of righteousness as a Tree of Life, bearing fruit that nourishes both the individual and the community. The theological implications of this verse suggest that righteous living reflects the life-giving nature of God and offers a form of spiritual nourishment that echoes the original Tree of Life in Eden. Through righteousness, believers participate in God's redemptive work, offering life to others and contributing to the restoration of creation.

For believers today, Proverbs 11:30 is a call to pursue righteousness and wisdom, not only for personal spiritual growth but to be a source of life and blessing to others. The fruit of righteousness is a tangible expression of God's life-giving power, and through it, we can reflect His character, contribute to the flourishing of our communities, and lead others toward the path of eternal life.

Proverbs 13:12: Hope Deferred and Its Contrast with the Tree of Life

In the book of Proverbs, the Tree of Life serves as a recurring symbol of life, fulfillment, and spiritual nourishment. However, the concept of the Tree of Life is also contrasted with life's experiences of frustration and delay, particularly when expectations are unmet. Proverbs 13:12 offers a striking comparison between hope that is deferred and the life-giving quality of fulfilled desires, which is likened to the Tree of Life:

"Hope deferred makes the heart sick, but a longing fulfilled is a tree of life." (Proverbs 13:12, NIV)

This verse highlights the emotional and spiritual tension that arises when our hopes and desires are delayed. It contrasts the disappointment and heartache caused by deferred hope with the joy and vitality that come when desires are fulfilled, which is symbolized by the Tree of Life. In this chapter, we will explore the implications of hope deferred, the significance of fulfilled desires, and the theological meaning behind the contrast with the Tree of Life.

Hope Deferred: The Pain of Unmet Expectations

1. The Nature of Hope in Proverbs:

- Hope as Expectation: In the biblical context, hope is not merely a wish or desire but carries a sense of expectation and confidence in the future. Hope is often rooted in trust in God's promises and the anticipation that He will bring about His purposes in the believer's life. Therefore, when hope is deferred—when what one longs for does not come to pass— it leads to deep emotional distress.

- The Heart's Sickness: The phrase "hope deferred makes the heart sick" captures the profound emotional impact of waiting for something that seems endlessly delayed. The heart, in biblical language, refers to the center of a person's emotional and spiritual life. When hope is continually postponed, it can lead to discouragement, despair, and even a sense of spiritual weariness. The longing for a better future or the fulfillment of a cherished desire, when unmet, can weigh heavily on the soul.

2. Examples of Deferred Hope in the Bible:

- Abraham and Sarah: A classic example of deferred hope in the Bible is the story of Abraham and Sarah, who waited decades for the fulfillment of God's promise that they would have a son (Genesis 12–21). Their years of waiting and the apparent impossibility of the promise being fulfilled in their old age likely caused them to experience the kind of "heart sickness" Proverbs 13:12 describes. Yet, when their longing was finally fulfilled with the birth of Isaac, it became a life-giving moment, akin to the Tree of Life.

- The Israelites in Exile: Another example is the experience of the Israelites in exile, waiting for the promised return to their homeland. The deferred hope of restoration to the Promised Land left them heartbroken and weary, as expressed in the lamentations of the prophets. Yet, their eventual return marked the fulfillment of long-held hopes, bringing new life to the nation.

The Fulfillment of Longing: A Tree of Life

1. The Joy of Fulfilled Desires:

- Longing Fulfilled as Life-Giving: The second half of Proverbs 13:12 offers a stark contrast to the heart sickness caused by deferred hope: "a longing fulfilled is a tree of life." The fulfillment of long-awaited desires is described in the most positive terms—likened to the Tree of Life, which symbolizes vitality, spiritual abundance, and divine blessing. Just as the Tree of Life in Genesis represents the fullness of life and communion with God, fulfilled longing brings a sense of completeness and joy, restoring the soul's vitality.

- The Tree of Life as a Metaphor: The use of the Tree of Life as a metaphor for fulfilled desires implies that when our longings are realized, we experience something akin to the divine life and blessing represented by the Tree of Life. It brings renewal, joy, and a sense of divine favor. The contrast between hope deferred and longing fulfilled shows how fulfillment transforms our emotional and spiritual state from discouragement to flourishing.

2. Theological Implications of Fulfilled Longing:

- Restoration and Healing: The Tree of Life in Proverbs 13:12 signifies the healing and restoration that come with fulfilled desires. Just as the Tree of Life in the new

Jerusalem in Revelation 22:2 is said to provide healing for the nations, fulfilled hopes and dreams have a healing effect on the heart and soul. This highlights the idea that God is a God of restoration—one who delights in fulfilling the desires of His people in ways that bring life and renewal.

- Foreshadowing of Ultimate Fulfillment: While this verse addresses the fulfillment of earthly desires, it also points to the ultimate fulfillment of all human longing in God's eschatological plan. Just as the Tree of Life in Eden was a sign of eternal life, the fulfillment of our longings in this life points to the future restoration of all things when we will once again have access to the Tree of Life in eternity (Revelation 22). The joys and satisfactions of this life, therefore, are a foretaste of the eternal life God offers through Christ.

Hope Deferred and Fulfilled Longing: Theological and Spiritual Lessons

1. The Struggle of Waiting:

- The Purpose of Deferred Hope: While deferred hope brings heartache, it also serves a spiritual purpose. Times of waiting can deepen a believer's trust in God and refine their faith. The Bible is filled with stories of individuals who experienced delayed fulfillment of God's promises, only to realize that God was shaping their character during the waiting period. The deferred hope teaches patience, perseverance, and dependence on God's timing rather than human expectations.

- Spiritual Growth through Waiting: Deferred hope, though painful, can be a season of spiritual growth. When we learn to trust God even when our desires are delayed, we develop a deeper reliance on Him. This reliance on God in the waiting period is often where transformation takes place, preparing us to fully appreciate the fulfillment when it finally comes.

2. The Joy of Fulfilled Hope:

- A Foretaste of Eternal Joy: When hope is fulfilled and desires are realized, it offers a glimpse of the eternal joy that awaits believers. Just as the Tree of Life symbolizes eternal life, fulfilled longings in this life provide a taste of the satisfaction and joy that will be complete in eternity. The realization of earthly hopes can remind us of God's ultimate promise to fulfill all longings in Christ, who is the true source of life.

- The Role of God's Promises: In Scripture, God's promises are central to the idea of hope. When we place our hope in God's promises, even in seasons of waiting, we can be assured that fulfillment will eventually come—whether in this life or the next. The promise of fulfilled hope through Christ is what sustains believers through times of deferred hope, knowing that God's timing is perfect and that His promises are sure.

Practical Applications for Believers

1. Trusting God in Seasons of Waiting:

- Patience and Perseverance: Proverbs 13:12 reminds believers that waiting for the fulfillment of hope can be difficult, but it also teaches the importance of patience and perseverance. Believers are called to trust in God's timing, knowing that He is working even in the delays. As we wait for the fulfillment of our hopes and desires, we must learn to lean on God's wisdom and trust that He knows what is best for us.

- Finding Strength in God's Promises: While waiting for hopes to be fulfilled, believers can find strength in the promises of God. His Word is filled with assurances that He is faithful, and even when our expectations are deferred, His purposes are always good. Holding onto these promises can prevent the heart from becoming "sick" during seasons of waiting.

2. Rejoicing in Fulfilled Longing:

- Gratitude for God's Provision: When longings are fulfilled, it is important to recognize them as blessings from God. Just as the Tree of Life was a gift of divine provision, fulfilled desires are a reflection of God's goodness and generosity. Believers are called to respond with gratitude and to share the joy of God's provision with others.

- Living in the Fullness of God's Blessings: Once desires are fulfilled, believers are invited to live in the fullness of those blessings, recognizing that God's provision brings life, joy, and flourishing. By embracing the gifts that come from fulfilled longings, believers reflect the life-giving nature of the Tree of Life in their own lives.

Proverbs 13:12 highlights the contrast between the heartache of deferred hope and the joy of fulfilled longing, using the powerful imagery of the Tree of Life. While waiting for hopes to be realized can be a painful process, the fulfillment of those hopes brings renewal and life. The Tree of Life symbolizes the vitality and joy that come when God's promises are fulfilled, offering a glimpse of the eternal life He promises to all believers.

For believers today, this verse serves as both a reminder of the challenges of waiting and an encouragement to trust in God's timing. The experience of deferred hope can shape our character, deepen our faith, and prepare us for the abundant life that comes when our longings are finally fulfilled. As we wait, we are invited to trust in God's goodness, knowing that every fulfilled desire is a foretaste of the ultimate life we will experience in His eternal kingdom.

Ecclesiastes 2:5: Symbolism of Trees and Their Meanings in Wisdom Literature

In the wisdom literature of the Bible, trees frequently symbolize life, prosperity, and divine blessing. Ecclesiastes 2:5 offers a glimpse into how trees are viewed symbolically in the context of human effort and the pursuit of fulfillment:

"I made myself gardens and parks, and planted in them all kinds of fruit trees."

(Ecclesiastes 2:5, ESV)

In this verse, King Solomon, traditionally considered the author of Ecclesiastes, describes his quest to find meaning through various pursuits, including the creation of gardens and the planting of trees. While on the surface this may seem like a simple reflection on horticultural projects, the deeper layers of wisdom literature often employ trees and gardens as symbols of broader existential and theological realities. Trees, in particular, serve as metaphors for the pursuit of life, the impermanence of earthly accomplishments, and the contrast between human striving and divine provision.

The Context of Ecclesiastes 2:5

1. The Search for Meaning in Life:

- Solomon's Experimentation with Pleasure: Ecclesiastes 2 recounts Solomon's quest to discover the purpose of life. Having been blessed with wisdom, wealth, and power, Solomon pursued every avenue of pleasure and accomplishment to find meaning, including the creation of grand works such as gardens and parks. His statement in verse 5 reflects his attempt to derive satisfaction and fulfillment through cultivating beauty and abundance in the world around him.

- Gardens and Trees as Symbols of Human Effort: The gardens and fruit trees that Solomon planted represent more than just aesthetic beauty; they symbolize human effort, creativity, and the desire to cultivate life and prosperity. However, as Ecclesiastes unfolds, it becomes clear that these projects, though impressive, do not provide lasting fulfillment. Solomon eventually concludes that all his efforts are "vanity" (Ecclesiastes 1:2), a Hebrew word meaning "breath" or "vapor," which reflects the transient nature of human achievements.

2. The Pursuit of Earthly Prosperity:

- Trees as Symbols of Prosperity: In the ancient world, and particularly in the wisdom literature, trees were often symbols of life, prosperity, and blessing. They provided food, shelter, and shade, making them essential to survival and flourishing. By planting fruit trees in his gardens, Solomon was engaging in an act that symbolized the human desire to create and sustain life. However, the very fact that he finds this pursuit ultimately unsatisfying reveals the limits of human effort to create lasting significance through material means.

- The Futility of Material Wealth: Ecclesiastes frequently contrasts the transience of earthly pursuits with the enduring nature of spiritual and eternal realities. While trees are enduring symbols of life and prosperity, Ecclesiastes 2:5 points to the reality that even the most beautiful and fruitful works of human hands—gardens and trees—cannot provide ultimate satisfaction. Solomon's reflection is that despite all his accomplishments, they were fleeting and left him longing for something more.

The Symbolism of Trees in Wisdom Literature

1. Trees as Symbols of Life and Longevity:

- The Tree of Life in Proverbs and Genesis: In other parts of wisdom literature, trees, particularly the Tree of Life, symbolize eternal life, divine wisdom, and spiritual vitality. The Tree of Life, which first appears in Genesis, represents the sustenance and eternal life that God provides. In Proverbs, the Tree of Life is used metaphorically to describe the life-giving nature of wisdom, righteousness, and fulfilled longing (Proverbs 3:18; 11:30; 13:12).

- Trees as Enduring Symbols: Trees are often seen as enduring, stable, and life-giving in a world that is otherwise subject to decay and change. In contrast to fleeting human accomplishments, trees can represent a connection to the eternal. In Ecclesiastes, however, Solomon's planting of trees, while meant to create a sense of permanence and legacy, is ultimately recognized as part of the ephemeral nature of life under the sun.

2. Trees as Symbols of Divine Blessing and Human Fragility:

- Prosperity and Blessing: Throughout the Bible, trees are often associated with divine blessing and provision. Psalm 1:3 famously compares a righteous person to "a tree planted by streams of water, which yields its fruit in season and whose leaf does not wither—whatever they do prospers." This image conveys the idea that those who live according to God's wisdom are nourished by a continual source of life and vitality, even in difficult circumstances. In this way, trees are symbols of prosperity and divine favor.

- Human Fragility: In Ecclesiastes, however, Solomon's reflection on the trees he planted underscores the temporary and fragile nature of human life. While trees are meant to be symbols of lasting life, Solomon's experience reveals that even the grandest human efforts are subject to time, decay, and futility. The fruit trees he planted, though life-giving, are ultimately bound by the same limitations as the rest of creation—they are temporary and cannot provide eternal fulfillment.

3. Gardens and Trees as Symbols of Paradise and Lost Fulfillment:

- Echoes of Eden: The imagery of gardens and trees in Ecclesiastes 2:5 echoes the Garden of Eden, where humanity first experienced life in perfect harmony with God. In Eden, trees represented God's provision, including the Tree of Life, which symbolized eternal communion with Him. By planting trees and creating gardens, Solomon may have been attempting to recreate a paradise-like environment—a place of beauty, abundance, and fulfillment. However, as Ecclesiastes reveals, such efforts, while noble, cannot restore what was lost in Eden. Human attempts to create paradise on earth are ultimately limited by the reality of sin, decay, and death.

- The Longing for Restoration: The gardens and trees Solomon planted reflect the human longing to return to a state of peace, prosperity, and fulfillment. Yet, Ecclesiastes highlights that this longing cannot be fully satisfied by human effort or material accomplishments. The symbolism of trees in wisdom literature thus points toward the need for divine restoration—a restoration that is ultimately fulfilled in God's future kingdom, where the Tree of Life reappears in the new Jerusalem (Revelation 22:2).

Theological Reflections on Trees and Human Ambition

1. The Limits of Human Achievement:

- Vanity and Transience: Ecclesiastes 2:5 serves as a reflection on the futility of human ambition when disconnected from a divine perspective. While trees symbolize life and prosperity, Solomon's ultimate realization is that even his greatest accomplishments are transient, like "chasing after the wind" (Ecclesiastes 1:14). The trees he planted, though fruitful and beautiful, are part of the impermanence of life under the sun.

- The Search for Meaning Beyond Material Success: The pursuit of material success and the creation of beauty, as symbolized by Solomon's trees and gardens, cannot provide lasting fulfillment. Ecclesiastes challenges readers to look beyond earthly achievements and to seek meaning in God, who alone can provide eternal life and satisfaction.

2. The Hope of Eternal Life:

- Trees as a Symbol of Eternal Life: While Ecclesiastes emphasizes the temporary nature of human endeavors, wisdom literature as a whole points to the enduring hope of eternal life. The Tree of Life, first seen in Genesis and reappearing in Revelation, represents God's promise of eternal life for those who trust in Him. While human accomplishments may fade, God's gift of eternal life remains, offering a lasting hope that transcends the limitations of this world.

- Fulfillment in God Alone: Ecclesiastes ultimately points to the conclusion that true fulfillment and meaning can only be found in God. The symbolic use of trees in wisdom literature underscores this message: just as trees are rooted in the ground and receive nourishment from the earth, so too must human beings be rooted in God's wisdom and provision in order to experience true life.

Ecclesiastes 2:5 offers a reflection on the symbolism of trees in the context of human ambition and the search for meaning. While trees are often seen as symbols of life, prosperity, and divine blessing in wisdom literature, Ecclesiastes presents a more sobering view: even the grandest human accomplishments, represented by gardens and fruit trees, are ultimately fleeting and incapable of providing lasting fulfillment.

Yet, the symbolism of trees in the Bible also points to the hope of eternal life and divine restoration. While human efforts may fail, God's promise of eternal life, symbolized by the Tree of Life, offers a lasting source of hope and meaning. For readers of Ecclesiastes, the lesson is clear: true fulfillment can only be found in God, who alone provides the life and satisfaction that transcend the vanity of earthly pursuits.

47

CHAPTER 03

THE TREE OF LIFE IN THE PROPHETS

Ezekiel 47:12: Vision of the River of Life and Trees Bearing Fruit

In the prophetic literature of the Bible, the imagery of trees and rivers frequently symbolizes renewal, divine provision, and the hope of restoration. One of the most vivid and theologically rich examples of this is found in Ezekiel 47, where the prophet describes a vision of a river flowing from the temple, nourishing trees whose fruit provides sustenance and healing. Ezekiel 47:12 reads:

"And on the banks, on both sides of the river, there will grow all kinds of trees for food. Their leaves will not wither, nor their fruit fail, but they will bear fresh fruit every month, because the water for them flows from the sanctuary. Their fruit will be for food, and their leaves for healing." (Ezekiel 47:12, ESV)

This prophetic vision evokes images reminiscent of the Tree of Life from Genesis, symbolizing God's provision and the hope for restoration. The vision not only reveals a future of abundance but also carries theological significance for understanding God's relationship with His people and His creation.

In this chapter, we will explore Ezekiel's vision in the context of the Tree of Life, examining its theological implications of restoration, healing, and eternal life.

Context of Ezekiel 47:12

1. The Prophetic Vision:

- Restoration After Exile: Ezekiel's prophecy occurs during a time of great distress for the people of Israel, who are in exile in Babylon after the destruction of Jerusalem and the temple. The vision described in Ezekiel 47 is part of a larger prophecy concerning the future restoration of the temple, the land, and God's people. This vision promises a time of renewal and divine blessing, when God will restore

His people and the land will once again flourish under His care.

- The River from the Temple: The river that Ezekiel sees flowing from the temple is not just a physical river but a symbol of the life-giving power of God's presence. The water flows from the sanctuary, the place where God's glory dwells, signifying that all life, healing, and abundance come directly from God. As the river flows, it transforms the surrounding landscape, bringing life to everything it touches, including the trees that bear fruit continuously.

2. The Symbolism of Trees in the Vision:

- Trees Along the Riverbank: In Ezekiel's vision, the trees along the banks of the river symbolize abundance and divine provision. These trees bear fruit every month, and their leaves do not wither. This represents an image of eternal sustenance, a direct result of the life-giving water flowing from the presence of God. These trees are reminiscent of the Tree of Life in the Garden of Eden, which also symbolized continuous life and divine provision.

- Healing and Nourishment: The fruit of these trees is described as food, and their leaves are for healing. This dual purpose emphasizes that God's provision is both physical and spiritual. The fruit nourishes the body, while the leaves heal, pointing to the wholeness that comes from God's restoration. This recalls the Tree of Life in Revelation 22:2, where the leaves are also described as being "for the healing of the nations," indicating a future time when God's restoration will be complete, bringing healing to all of creation.

Theological Implications of Ezekiel 47:12

1. Restoration and Renewal:

- God as the Source of Life: The river flowing from the temple and nourishing the trees is a powerful image of God's life-giving presence. In Ezekiel's vision, it is God's presence that transforms the barren land into a place of abundance. This reflects the theological theme that God alone is the source of true life. Just as the river brings life to the trees, God's presence brings life to His people and all of creation. This points to the future hope of restoration after Israel's exile and, more broadly, to the ultimate restoration of all things in God's kingdom.

- A Return to Eden: The imagery of trees bearing fruit continuously and leaves providing healing echoes the Tree of Life in the Garden of Eden. In Eden, the Tree of Life symbolized eternal life and the provision of God before the fall of humanity. Ezekiel's vision of these trees suggests a return to the abundance of Eden—a time when the brokenness caused by sin will be healed, and God's people will once again enjoy the fullness of His provision. This prophetic vision anticipates a future restoration of the relationship between God and humanity, where creation is fully renewed.

2. Healing for the Nations:

- Leaves for Healing: One of the most profound aspects of Ezekiel's vision is that the leaves of the trees are described as being for healing. This indicates that God's restorative power is not limited to physical nourishment but extends to spiritual and emotional healing as well. The fact that the trees are continually fruitful and their leaves provide ongoing healing suggests a time when all the wounds of the world—spiritual, emotional, and physical—will be healed through God's presence.

- Foreshadowing the New Jerusalem: Ezekiel's vision is echoed in the final chapters of Revelation, where the Tree of Life reappears in the new Jerusalem. Revelation 22:1-2 describes the river of the water of life flowing from the throne of God and the Lamb, and on either side of the river is the Tree of Life, bearing fruit each month and with leaves for the healing of the nations. This parallel between Ezekiel and Revelation points to the ultimate fulfillment of God's plan for the world—a time when His presence will bring complete healing and restoration, not just for Israel but for all nations.

3. Perpetual Provision:

- Fruit for Food: The trees bear fruit every month, a sign of perpetual provision. In the ancient Near East, fruit-bearing trees were seasonal, but in Ezekiel's vision, the trees are continually producing fruit, symbolizing the unending provision of God. This reflects the nature of God's blessings: they are not occasional or limited but abundant and constant. God's provision is not subject to seasons or circumstances; He is continually present to sustain His people.

- Spiritual Sustenance: While the vision of trees bearing fruit can be understood literally as physical nourishment, it also has deeper spiritual significance. The fruit of these trees represents the spiritual sustenance that comes from living in the presence of God. Just as the water from the temple nourishes the trees, God's presence nourishes the soul, providing what is needed for spiritual growth and flourishing.

The Tree of Life in Prophetic Visions

1. Ezekiel's Trees and the Tree of Life in Revelation:

- Common Themes of Life and Healing: The trees in Ezekiel 47 and the Tree of Life in Revelation 22 share common themes of life, healing, and divine provision. Both sets of trees are fed by a life-giving river that flows from God's presence, and both produce fruit that sustains life and leaves that heal. This continuity in imagery suggests that the Tree of Life is not just a past reality from the Garden of Eden but a future promise of restoration, where God's people will once again experience the fullness of life in His presence.

- Eschatological Hope: Ezekiel's vision points forward to the eschatological hope of the new creation, where all things will be made new and God's people will live in harmony with Him. The trees in Ezekiel's vision foreshadow the return of the Tree of Life in the new Jerusalem, where the effects of sin and death will be no more, and humanity will be fully restored to life as God intended.

2. The Symbolism of the River of Life:

- Water as a Symbol of Life and Purification: Throughout the Bible, water is often used as a symbol of life, purification, and the presence of the Holy Spirit. In Ezekiel's vision, the river flowing from the temple represents the outpouring of God's presence, which brings life wherever it flows. This is similar to the imagery in Revelation, where the river of the water of life flows from the throne of God. Both images emphasize that true life comes from being in the presence of God and receiving His Spirit, which cleanses, sustains, and gives life.

- Spiritual Renewal: The river in Ezekiel's vision transforms the landscape, bringing life to what was once barren and dead. This symbolizes the spiritual renewal that comes when God's presence flows into the lives of His people. Just as the river brings physical renewal to the trees, God's Spirit brings spiritual renewal to the hearts of believers, enabling them to bear fruit and flourish in their walk with Him.

Practical Implications for Believers Today

1. Trusting in God's Provision:

- God as Our Source: Ezekiel 47:12 reminds us that God is the ultimate source of all life and provision. Just as the trees along the riverbank flourish because of the water that flows from the temple, we can only flourish when we remain connected to God and draw our sustenance from Him. In times of spiritual dryness or uncertainty, we are called to trust in God's provision, knowing that He is able to nourish and sustain us both physically and spiritually.

2. Healing and Restoration in God's Presence:

- Healing for the Broken: The leaves of the trees in Ezekiel's vision provide healing, reminding us that God's presence has the power to heal the deepest wounds—whether they be physical, emotional, or spiritual. For believers today, this is a powerful reminder that no matter what brokenness or pain we experience, God's healing power is available to us through His Spirit and His presence. We can turn to Him for restoration, trusting that His healing is continual and complete.

Ezekiel 47:12 presents a powerful vision of life, healing, and restoration, centered on the imagery of trees nourished by the river of life flowing from the temple. These trees, bearing fruit every month and offering leaves for healing, echo the Tree of Life from Genesis and foreshadow the ultimate restoration described in Revelation. Ezekiel's vision provides hope not only for the immediate restoration of Israel but also for the future renewal of all creation, when God's presence will once again bring life and healing to the world.

For believers today, Ezekiel's vision serves as a reminder of God's continual provision, His power to heal and restore, and the hope of eternal life in His presence. The Tree of Life, which was once lost in Eden, will one day be restored, and through Christ, we can experience the life-giving power of God even now.

Joel 2:22: The Restoration of Nature and Its Implications

The prophetic book of Joel focuses on themes of judgment, repentance, and restoration. Joel 2:22, in particular, addresses the restoration of nature as part of God's redemptive plan for His people and the land:

"Do not be afraid, you wild animals, for the pastures in the wilderness are becoming green. The trees are bearing their fruit; the fig tree and the vine yield their riches." (Joel 2:22, NIV)

This verse is a powerful depiction of the restoration of the natural world as a consequence of God's mercy and blessing. It forms part of a broader prophetic vision where, after a period of destruction and desolation, God's renewal of both the people and the land brings forth life and abundance. The imagery of trees bearing fruit and the natural world flourishing is rich with theological and symbolic significance, reflecting not only the physical restoration of the land but also spiritual renewal and divine blessing.

In this chapter, we will explore the restoration of nature as portrayed in Joel 2:22, examining its symbolic meaning and theological implications for humanity, creation, and the ultimate fulfillment of God's redemptive purposes.

Context of Joel 2:22

1. The Crisis in Joel's Prophecy:

- A Time of Destruction: Joel begins with a vivid description of devastation brought by a plague of locusts, which serves as a metaphor for divine judgment upon the people of Israel. This judgment is portrayed as total, affecting both the land and the people. The locusts strip the land of its vegetation, leaving it barren and lifeless, and the drought compounds the devastation. This imagery underscores the connection between human sin and the disruption of the natural order.

- Call to Repentance: In response to this catastrophe, Joel calls the people to repentance, urging them to turn back to God with fasting and prayer (Joel 2:12-13). The destruction of the land mirrors the spiritual desolation of the people, and only through genuine repentance can restoration begin. The connection between the state of the land and the people's relationship with God emphasizes the intertwined fate of humanity and nature in the biblical worldview.

2. The Promise of Restoration:

- God's Response: After the call to repentance, Joel proclaims that God, in His mercy, will restore what has been lost. Joel 2:21 declares that the people should not fear, for God will "do great things." This is immediately followed by the reassurance given to the land and animals in Joel 2:22. God's act of restoration will not only bless the people but also renew the natural world, which has suffered as a consequence of human sin.

- Restoration of the Land: The restoration of nature is central to the vision of hope that Joel presents. The pastures that had been devastated by the locusts are now "becoming green," the trees that had been barren are "bearing their fruit," and the fig tree and vine are producing their riches. This imagery of abundance reflects a complete reversal of the earlier judgment. The natural world, which had suffered under the weight of divine judgment, is now flourishing as a result of God's redemptive work.

Theological Implications of the Restoration of Nature

1. The Interconnectedness of Humanity and Creation:

- Creation Suffering from Human Sin: The devastation of nature in Joel's prophecy is directly linked to the people's sin and rebellion against God. Throughout Scripture, human sin is shown to have consequences not only for individuals but for the land and creation itself. In Genesis 3, after Adam and Eve's disobedience, the ground is cursed, and nature experiences the effects of the fall. Similarly, in Joel, the desolation of the land reflects the spiritual condition of the people.

- Nature's Restoration Tied to Repentance: The restoration of the natural world in Joel 2:22 highlights the biblical principle that creation is deeply affected by humanity's relationship with God. As the people repent and turn back to God, the land, too, is renewed. This reflects the broader biblical theme that God's redemption extends not only to humanity but to all of creation. The flourishing of nature is a sign of God's blessing and the restoration of right relationships between humanity, creation, and the Creator.

2. The Role of Nature in Divine Blessing:

- Trees Bearing Fruit as a Sign of Divine Favor: The imagery of trees bearing fruit in Joel 2:22 symbolizes the return of God's favor and blessing. In the Bible, trees are often associated with life, prosperity, and divine provision. The fact that the fig tree and vine are yielding their "riches" signals a return to the Edenic vision of abundance, where God's creation flourishes under His care. This abundance is not merely physical but also points to spiritual renewal, where the people experience the fullness of God's blessings.

- The Earth as an Agent of God's Redemption: The restoration of nature in Joel suggests that the natural world plays an active role in God's redemptive purposes. The renewal of the land is a tangible expression of God's mercy and a sign of the larger restoration that He is bringing about. The earth itself participates in the redemption of God's people, flourishing as they are restored to right relationship with their Creator. This reflects the biblical vision of a harmonious relationship between humanity and the earth, which will ultimately be fully realized in the new creation.

3. Eschatological Implications: The New Creation:

- Foreshadowing the New Creation: Joel's vision of the restoration of nature points forward to the eschatological hope of the new creation. In Revelation 21 and 22, we see the ultimate fulfillment of God's redemptive purposes, where the new heaven and new earth are revealed. The Tree of Life, which first appeared in Eden, reappears in the new Jerusalem, bearing fruit for the healing of the nations. The renewal of the natural world in Joel is a foretaste of this final restoration, where creation itself will be fully redeemed and restored.

- Creation's Groaning for Redemption: The Apostle Paul echoes this theme in Romans 8:19-22, where he speaks of creation "groaning" in anticipation of its liberation from the effects of sin. Just as humanity awaits the final redemption, so too does creation long for the day when it will be restored to its original purpose. The restoration of nature in Joel 2:22 serves as a reminder that God's redemptive plan includes all of creation, not just humanity.

Restoration of Nature as a Symbol of Spiritual Renewal

1. Nature Reflecting Spiritual Realities:

- The Land as a Mirror of the People's Condition: In Joel, the state of the land is closely tied to the spiritual condition of the people. When the people are in rebellion, the land is desolate and barren. When the people repent and return to God, the land flourishes and bears fruit. This connection between the natural and spiritual realms highlights the idea that creation often reflects the spiritual realities of humanity's relationship with God.

- Abundance as a Sign of God's Presence: The restoration of the land in Joel 2:22 is a sign of God's renewed presence among His people. Just as the trees bear fruit and the pastures become green, so too does the people's relationship with God experience renewal and growth. The abundance of the natural world serves as a visible representation of the spiritual abundance that comes from living in harmony with God's will.

2. The Healing Power of God's Restoration:

- Healing of the Land and the People: The renewal of nature in Joel is not just about the physical restoration of the land; it also points to the healing of the people's relationship with God. As the land flourishes, it reflects the healing and restoration that God is bringing to His people. The natural world becomes a symbol of the deeper spiritual renewal that takes place when God's people turn back to Him in repentance and faith.

- The Tree of Life as a Symbol of Healing: The imagery of trees bearing fruit in Joel 2:22 is reminiscent of the

Tree of Life, which provides healing in Revelation 22. Just as the fruit of the Tree of Life brings healing to the nations, the trees in Joel's vision symbolize the healing and restoration that come through God's redemptive work. This healing extends beyond the physical realm to include the spiritual and emotional healing of the people, as they are restored to right relationship with their Creator.

Practical Implications for Believers Today

1. Caring for Creation as Part of God's Redemptive Plan:

- Human Responsibility in Stewardship: Joel 2:22 reminds believers that creation is an integral part of God's redemptive plan. As such, believers are called to care for the earth and participate in its renewal. The flourishing of the land in Joel's prophecy reflects the broader biblical theme that humanity is entrusted with the stewardship of creation. As we await the final restoration of all things, we are called to be responsible caretakers of the earth, recognizing that our actions affect not only the environment but also reflect our relationship with God.

- Environmental Restoration as a Reflection of Spiritual Renewal: Just as the land in Joel is restored when the people turn back to God, believers today are called to see the care of creation as part of their spiritual calling. The health of the environment can serve as a reflection of humanity's spiritual health, and believers are called to live in ways that promote the flourishing of both the naturaland spiritual realms.

2. Hope in God's Power to Restore:

- Trusting in God's Promise of Renewal: Joel 2:22 offers a message of hope for believers, reminding us that God is able to bring restoration to even the most desolate places. Whether in our personal lives, our communities, or the world at large, we can trust in God's power to restore and renew. The flourishing of nature in Joel's vision is a reminder that no situation is beyond God's ability to redeem, and that His purposes for creation and humanity will ultimately be fulfilled.

- Looking Forward to the New Creation: The restoration of nature in Joel also points believers forward to the hope of the new creation, where all things will be made new. As we experience glimpses of God's restoration in this life, we are reminded of the ultimate restoration that is yet to come. This hope sustains believers in times of difficulty and encourages us to live in anticipation of the day when God's kingdom will be fully realized.

Joel 2:22 presents a powerful vision of the restoration of nature as part of God's redemptive plan. The flourishing of the land, the trees bearing fruit, and the abundance of the natural world all point to the renewal that comes when God's people turn back to Him in repentance. This restoration not only reflects physical renewal but also symbolizes the deeper spiritual healing and renewal that come from being in right relationship with God.

For believers today, the restoration of nature in Joel offers hope and encouragement. It reminds us that God's redemptive purposes extend to all of creation, and that we are called to participate in His work of renewal. As we care for the earth and live in harmony with God's will, we reflect the abundant life that He offers, both now and in the future when all things will be restored in the new creation.

Isaiah 55:12: The Joy of Nature's Restoration and Its Connection to Life

In Isaiah 55, the prophet Isaiah proclaims a message of hope and restoration, addressing a people who have faced exile, loss, and brokenness. As part of this vision of renewal, Isaiah 55:12 offers a vivid description of the joy that accompanies the restoration of nature, which reflects the broader spiritual restoration of God's people:

"You will go out in joy and be led forth in peace; the mountains and hills will burst into song before you, and all the trees of the field will clap their hands."

(Isaiah 55:12, NIV)

This verse paints a beautiful picture of the natural world rejoicing alongside humanity, celebrating the redemption and renewal that God brings. It connects the restoration of nature to the life-giving power of God's word and the fulfillment of His promises. The imagery of trees clapping their hands and mountains singing reflects the interconnectedness of humanity and creation in experiencing the joy of God's redemption.

In this chapter, we will explore the theological significance of Isaiah 55:12, examining the joy that comes with the restoration of nature and its connection to the abundant life that God offers His people.

Context of Isaiah 55:12

1. The Call to Return to God:

- Isaiah 55's Invitation: The broader chapter of Isaiah 55 is an invitation to come and receive the life that only God can give. It opens with an appeal to the thirsty and hungry to come and be satisfied, not by earthly provisions but by the spiritual sustenance that God freely offers (Isaiah 55:1-3). This chapter represents a turning point, where God promises His people that, despite their past unfaithfulness and exile, He is offering them a new covenant, a fresh opportunity to live in His presence and enjoy His blessings.

- God's Word Accomplishing Its Purpose: Isaiah 55:10-11 speaks of God's word being like rain that waters the earth, bringing forth life and growth. Just as rain fulfills its purpose in causing the earth to produce crops, so too does God's word accomplish His will, bringing life and restoration to His people. This sets the stage for verse 12, where the joy of nature's restoration mirrors the joy of the people as they experience the fulfillment of God's promises.

2. The Promise of Joy and Peace:

- Going Out in Joy: Isaiah 55:12 begins with a promise that God's people "will go out in joy and be led forth in peace." This reflects the hope of restoration after exile, where God's people will be released from bondage and experience a renewed sense of joy, peace, and freedom. Their journey is not just a physical return to their land but a spiritual renewal that is marked by joy and harmony with God.

- Nature's Participation in Redemption: What is striking about this verse is that the joy of restoration is not limited to humanity alone; creation itself participates in the celebration. The mountains and hills "burst into song" and the trees "clap their hands," symbolizing the harmonious relationship between humanity and the natural world when God's redemption is realized. This is a vision of cosmic renewal, where all of creation rejoices in God's saving work.

Theological Implications of the Restoration of Nature

1. Nature as a Participant in God's Redemption:

- Creation Rejoicing in God's Work: Isaiah 55:12 presents nature as an active participant in the joy of God's redemptive work. The imagery of mountains singing and trees clapping their hands conveys the idea that all of creation is interconnected with humanity and shares in the blessings of God's restoration. This reflects the broader biblical theme that creation, which was affected by the fall (Genesis 3), will ultimately be restored to its original purpose as part of God's redemptive plan.

- Restoration of Harmony Between Humanity and Creation: In Isaiah's vision, the restoration of humanity leads to the restoration of the natural world. This echoes the original harmony between humanity and creation in the Garden of Eden, where humanity was tasked with caring for and tending the earth (Genesis 2:15). The joy and peace described in Isaiah 55:12 point to a time when this relationship will be fully restored, and humanity will once again live in harmony with the natural world under God's reign.

2. Nature as a Symbol of Spiritual Renewal:

- Trees as Symbols of Life: In the Bible, trees often symbolize life, growth, and divine provision. The trees "clapping their hands" in Isaiah 55:12 represent the flourishing of life that comes with God's restoration. This imagery ties back to the Tree of Life in Genesis, which symbolized eternal life and God's ongoing provision for His people. Just as the Tree of Life was a source of nourishment and vitality, the restored trees in Isaiah's vision symbolize the abundant life that God brings to His people.

- Joy in God's Presence: The joy of nature's restoration mirrors the joy that comes from being in the presence of God. Just as the trees clap their hands and the mountains burst into song, God's people are invited to join in the celebration of His goodness and faithfulness. This joy is not merely emotional but reflects the deep sense of peace and fulfillment that comes from living in alignment with God's will and experiencing His salvation.

The Connection Between Nature's Restoration and Life

1. God's Word as the Source of Life:

- The Power of God's Word: Isaiah 55:10-11 emphasizes the life-giving power of God's word, which is compared to rain that nourishes the earth and causes it to bring forth life. This analogy highlights the idea that just as rain is essential for physical life, God's word is essential for spiritual life. It accomplishes God's purposes and brings about the transformation and renewal that He intends.

- Life Abundant Through God's Promise: The restoration of nature described in verse 12 reflects the abundant life that flows from God's word. As the trees clap their hands and the hills sing, they embody the life and vitality that come from being connected to the source of all life— God Himself. This points to the idea that true life, both for humanity and creation, is found in relationship with God and in the fulfillment of His promises.

2. Creation's Role in the New Creation:

- Foreshadowing the New Creation: The restoration of nature in Isaiah 55:12 points forward to the eschatological hope of the new creation, where God's people and creation will be fully restored. This theme is picked up in Revelation 21 and 22, where the new heaven and new earth are revealed, and the Tree of Life reappears, providing healing for the nations (Revelation 22:2). In the new creation, nature will no longer be subject to decay and suffering but will flourish in the presence of God, just as it does in Isaiah's vision.

- Creation Groaning for Redemption: The Apostle Paul reflects on this in Romans 8:19-22, where he describes creation as "groaning" in anticipation of its liberation from the effects of sin. Just as humanity awaits the fulfillment of God's promises, so too does creation long for the day when it will be restored to its original glory. The joy of nature's restoration in Isaiah 55:12 is a foretaste of the ultimate renewal that will come when God's kingdom is fully established.

Practical Implications for Believers Today

1. Living in Harmony with Creation:

- Stewardship of Creation: Isaiah 55:12 reminds believers of the interconnectedness between humanity and the natural world. As God's people, we are called to be good stewards of creation, caring for the earth and promoting its flourishing. The vision of nature rejoicing in God's restoration challenges us to consider how our actions impact the environment and to live in ways that reflect God's care for all of creation.

- Participating in God's Redemptive Work: Just as nature rejoices in God's restoration, believers are invited to participate in His redemptive work by promoting justice, peace, and healing in the world. As we work to restore broken relationships, care for the environment, and live in harmony with God's will, we reflect the joy and peace that Isaiah describes. This joy is not just for the future but can be experienced now as we live in alignment with God's purposes.

2. Experiencing the Joy of Restoration:

- Joy in God's Salvation: The joy described in Isaiah 55:12 is a reflection of the joy that comes from experiencing God's salvation. As believers, we are invited to "go out in joy" and to live with a deep sense of peace, knowing that God has redeemed us and is working to restore all things. This joy is not dependent on circumstances but flows from the knowledge that God's word will accomplish His purposes and that we are part of His redemptive plan.

- Hope for the Future: Isaiah's vision of nature's restoration points to the hope of the new creation, where all things will be made new. As believers, we can look forward to the day when God's kingdom will be fully realized, and we will experience the joy of living in perfect harmony with God, creation, and one another. This hope sustains us in times of difficulty and gives us a sense of purpose as we work toward the fulfillment of God's promises.

Isaiah 55:12 offers a powerful vision of the joy that comes with the restoration of nature, which is closely connected to the life-giving power of God's word and the fulfillment of His promises. The imagery of mountains singing and trees clapping their hands reflects the harmonious relationship between humanity and creation when God's redemption is realized. This restoration of nature is not only a physical renewal but also a symbol of the spiritual renewal that comes through God's salvation.

For believers today, Isaiah's vision provides both hope and a call to action. We are invited to live in harmony with creation, to participate in God's redemptive work, and to experience the joy and peace that come from living in alignment with His will. As we look forward to the ultimate restoration of all things in the new creation, we can find joy in knowing that God's promises are sure and that His word will accomplish all that He intends.

CHAPTER 04

THE TREE OF LIFE IN THE NEW TESTAMENT

Revelation 2:7: Promise of Eating from the Tree of Life in Paradise

In the New Testament, the Tree of Life reappears as a symbol of eternal life and divine blessing, particularly in the book of Revelation. Revelation 2:7 contains a significant promise to those who overcome:

"Whoever has ears, let them hear what the Spirit says to the churches. To the one who is victorious, I will give the right to eat from the tree of life, which is in the paradise of God."

(Revelation 2:7, NIV)

This verse comes as part of the message to the church in Ephesus and contains a powerful promise of reward for the faithful. The image of the Tree of Life in paradise, a place of eternal communion with God, echoes the Tree of Life in the Garden of Eden and carries with it deep theological implications for the believer's ultimate destiny.

In this chapter, we will explore the meaning of Revelation 2:7, focusing on the promise of eating from the Tree of Life, its connection to paradise, and the significance of this reward for believers. The restoration of access to the Tree of Life in the new creation serves as a powerful conclusion to the biblical narrative, symbolizing the fulfillment of God's redemptive plan and the eternal life He offers to His people.

Context of Revelation 2:7

1. The Message to the Church in Ephesus:

- The Call to Faithfulness: Revelation 2:7 is part of the message to the church in Ephesus, one of the seven churches addressed in the opening chapters of Revelation. The church in Ephesus is commended for its hard work and perseverance but is also warned about losing its "first love"

(Revelation 2:4). The call to repentance and renewal is coupled with a promise for those who overcome, signaling that faithfulness will lead to great reward.

- The Overcomers: The phrase "to the one who is victorious" refers to those who remain faithful to Christ despite challenges and opposition. Revelation consistently emphasizes the importance of overcoming—remaining steadfast in faith in the face of trials and temptations. The promise of eating from the Tree of Life is reserved for these "overcomers," those who persevere and remain loyal to Christ.

2. The Tree of Life in Paradise:

- Return to the Garden of Eden: The Tree of Life in Revelation 2:7 evokes the imagery of the Tree of Life in the Garden of Eden, from which humanity was barred after the fall (Genesis 3:22-24). The loss of access to the Tree of Life represented humanity's separation from God and the forfeiture of eternal life. By promising access to the Tree of Life in paradise, Revelation points to the restoration of what was lost—eternal life and communion with God.

- Paradise Restored: The term "paradise" used in this verse reflects a return to the Edenic state of perfect harmony between God, humanity, and creation. The Greek word for paradise (παράδεισος, paradeisos) refers to a garden or park, evoking the imagery of Eden. In this context, paradise represents the eternal dwelling place of God's people, where they will live in His presence and enjoy the fullness of life.

Theological Implications of Eating from the Tree of Life

1. Restoration of Eternal Life:

- Reversing the Effects of the Fall: The promise of eating from the Tree of Life in Revelation 2:7 is a profound symbol of the reversal of the effects of the fall. In Genesis 3, after Adam and Eve sinned, they were expelled from the Garden of Eden, and access to the Tree of Life was cut off. This separation symbolized humanity's loss of eternal life and direct fellowship with God. Revelation 2:7 points to the ultimate restoration of that fellowship, where the faithful are granted access to the Tree of Life once again.

- Eternal Communion with God: Eating from the Tree of Life in paradise signifies eternal life in the presence of God. In the same way that Adam and Eve were meant to enjoy eternal communion with God in Eden, those who overcome in Christ are promised this restored relationship. The Tree of Life serves as a symbol of God's provision of eternal sustenance, life, and joy for His people.

2. The Reward for Overcomers:

- Faithfulness Rewarded: Revelation 2:7 emphasizes that the reward of eating from the Tree of Life is reserved for those who are victorious in their faith. This reward is not automatic but is given to those who remain steadfast in their commitment to Christ. The imagery of the Tree of Life, with its associations of eternal blessing, highlights the magnitude of this reward—it is the gift of eternal life, symbolizing the ultimate victory over sin, death, and separation from God.

- The Power of Christ's Victory: The promise of eternal life through the Tree of Life is made possible by the victory of Christ. His death and resurrection defeated the powers of sin and death, making it possible for believers to overcome as well. In this way, the Tree of Life is not merely a future promise but is already accessible through faith in Christ, who offers eternal life to all who believe in Him (John 10:28).

3. The Tree of Life as a Symbol of Divine Provision:

- Sustenance and Abundance: The Tree of Life is not just a symbol of eternal life but also of divine provision. In Eden, the Tree of Life represented God's ongoing sustenance and blessing for Adam and Eve, providing them with everything they needed to flourish in God's presence. In Revelation, this same tree is a symbol of the abundance of life that God offers to His people in eternity. The act of eating from the Tree of Life signifies being nourished and sustained by God's presence forever.

- A Continuous Source of Life: The Tree of Life in paradise represents the continual provision of life and blessing that flows from God. Just as the tree in Eden was a source of unending life, the Tree of Life in Revelation symbolizes the everlasting life that the faithful will enjoy in God's presence. It is a reminder that God is the ultimate source of life and that He will provide for His people for all eternity.

The Tree of Life in the Broader Context of Revelation

1. The Tree of Life in the New Jerusalem:

- Revelation 22:2 and the Healing of the Nations: The Tree of Life appears again in Revelation 22:2, where it is situated in the New Jerusalem. In this final vision, the tree grows on both sides of the river of the water of life, and its leaves are for the healing of the nations. This imagery reinforces the idea that the Tree of Life is a symbol of divine healing, restoration, and life. The nations, once divided and broken by sin, are now healed and brought into the fullness of God's kingdom.

- Access to the Tree of Life Restored: In the New Jerusalem, access to the Tree of Life is no longer restricted, as it was in Eden. Revelation 22:14 blesses those who "wash their robes" so that they "may have the right to the tree of life and may go through the gates into the city." This indicates that, through Christ's redemptive work, the faithful now have access to eternal life and to the full blessings of God's kingdom.

2. Eschatological Fulfillment:

- A Symbol of Final Restoration: The Tree of Life in Revelation symbolizes the final restoration of all things. It serves as a bookend to the biblical narrative, beginning in Genesis as a symbol of eternal life in the Garden of Eden and reappearing in Revelation as a sign of the ultimate fulfillment of God's promises. The Tree of Life in the New Jerusalem represents the culmination of God's redemptive work, where creation is renewed, and humanity is restored to full fellowship with God.

- A Foretaste of the Kingdom: While the Tree of Life is fully realized in the eschatological future, its promise is already available to believers through faith in Christ. The eternal life that the Tree of Life symbolizes is not just a future hope but something that believers can begin to experience now. Through the indwelling of the Holy Spirit, believers have access to the life of the kingdom and can live in the assurance of God's eternal provision.

Practical Implications for Believers Today

1. Living as Overcomers:

- Faithfulness in the Face of Trials: Revelation 2:7 encourages believers to remain faithful to Christ, even in the face of opposition, temptation, and hardship. The promise of eating from the Tree of Life serves as a motivation to persevere, knowing that the reward for faithfulness is eternal life in God's presence. Believers are called to live as overcomers, trusting in God's strength to sustain them through life's challenges.

- Hope in the Promise of Eternal Life: The promise of eating from the Tree of Life gives believers a future hope that sustains them in the present. Knowing that eternal life awaits those who overcome provides a perspective that helps believers endure suffering and remain steadfast in their faith. This hope is not just for the distant future but is a living reality that shapes how believers live today.

2. Experiencing God's Provision Now:

- Spiritual Nourishment in Christ: The Tree of Life is a symbol of the abundant life that God offers through Christ. Believers are invited to experience this

life now through a relationship with Christ, who provides spiritual nourishment, strength, and guidance. Just as the Tree of Life in paradise represents the fullness of life in God's presence, Christ offers a foretaste of this eternal life through the Holy Spirit, who sustains believers in their daily walk.

- Living in Anticipation of God's Kingdom: The promise of eternal life calls believers to live in anticipation of God's kingdom. As citizens of the kingdom of God, believers are called to live in a way that reflects the values of the kingdom—justice, peace, love, and righteousness. The Tree of Life is a reminder that the life of the kingdom is already breaking into the present, and believers are called to participate in God's redemptive work here and now.

Revelation 2:7 offers a profound promise of eternal life to those who overcome in their faith. The imagery of eating from the Tree of Life in paradise evokes the biblical story of creation, fall, and restoration, pointing to the fulfillment of God's redemptive plan. The Tree of Life, which was once lost to humanity due to sin, is now restored through the victory of Christ, who offers eternal life to all who believe in Him.

For believers today, the promise of eating from the Tree of Life serves as both a future hope and a present reality. It reminds us of the eternal life that awaits us in God's presence and calls us to live faithfully in anticipation of His kingdom. As we persevere in faith, we are invited to experience the abundant life that God offers, knowing that the fullness of this life will be realized in the new creation.

Revelation 22:2: The Tree of Life in the New Jerusalem and Its Healing Properties

In the closing chapters of the Bible, the book of Revelation offers a majestic vision of the new heaven and the new earth, culminating in the depiction of the New Jerusalem.

In this vision, the Tree of Life reappears, symbolizing the restoration of everything lost due to sin and the fulfillment of God's redemptive plan. Revelation 22:2 describes the Tree of Life in the new Jerusalem:

"On each side of the river stood the tree of life, bearing twelve crops of fruit, yielding its fruit every month. And the leaves of the tree are for the healing of the nations."

(Revelation 22:2, NIV)

This image of the Tree of Life, located on either side of the river of life, emphasizes its role in providing eternal sustenance and healing for all of creation. It is a powerful symbol of the complete restoration of humanity and nature, as well as the eternal life that believers will enjoy in God's presence.

In this chapter, we will explore the significance of the Tree of Life in the New Jerusalem as depicted in Revelation 22:2, focusing on its symbolism, the meaning of its healing properties, and its role in God's ultimate plan for redemption and restoration.

Context of Revelation 22:2

1. The Vision of the New Jerusalem:

- Revelation's Final Vision: Revelation 22:2 occurs within the final vision of the new Jerusalem, which represents the culmination of God's redemptive plan for humanity and creation. After the defeat of evil, the new heaven and new earth are revealed, and the New Jerusalem descends as the eternal dwelling place of God with His people (Revelation 21:1-4). This city is a place of perfect communion between God and His creation, where death, mourning, and pain no longer exist.

- The River of Life: Central to this vision is the river of the water of life, which flows from the throne of God and the Lamb. The river represents the life-giving presence of God, flowing from His throne and nourishing everything in its path. The imagery of the river of life recalls the Garden of Eden, where a river flowed to water the garden (Genesis 2:10). In the new Jerusalem, the river signifies the restoration of divine life and the abundance of God's provision.

2. The Tree of Life in the New Jerusalem:

- The Return of the Tree of Life: The Tree of Life reappears in Revelation 22, having been absent since Genesis. In Eden, the Tree of Life symbolized eternal life and communion with God, but access to it was lost due to sin (Genesis 3:22-24). Its return in the new Jerusalem signals the restoration of eternal life for humanity and the fulfillment of God's original intention for creation. The presence of the Tree of Life in the new Jerusalem marks the full realization of God's plan of salvation.

- Location and Function: The Tree of Life in Revelation 22:2 is described as growing on either side of the river of the water of life. This suggests that the Tree of Life is not limited to one place but is abundant and accessible to all. Its constant fruit-bearing and healing properties indicate its role as a source of continuous life and blessing for all who dwell in the new Jerusalem.

Theological Implications of the Tree of Life in Revelation 22:2

1. Eternal Life and Divine Provision:

- Twelve Crops of Fruit: The Tree of Life is described as bearing twelve crops of fruit, yielding fruit every month. This imagery emphasizes the tree's role as a source of ongoing nourishment and life. The number twelve is often symbolic in the Bible, representing completeness and perfection (e.g., the twelve tribes of Israel, the twelve apostles). The twelve crops of fruit suggest that God's provision is perfect and abundant, fully meeting the needs of His people.

- Continuous Sustenance: The fact that the tree yields fruit every month points to the unending nature of God's provision. Unlike the seasonal cycles of earthly trees, the Tree of Life bears fruit continually, symbolizing the eternal life that flows from God. In the new Jerusalem, there is no lack or scarcity—God's people will be sustained forever by His life-giving presence.

2. Healing for the Nations:

- The Healing of the Nations: One of the most striking aspects of the Tree of Life in Revelation 22:2 is that its leaves are for the "healing of the nations." This imagery suggests that the restoration offered by the Tree of Life is not only physical but also spiritual and relational. The nations, often divided by sin, conflict, and strife, are now healed and united in the presence of God.

- Restoration of All Things: The healing of the nations points to the full restoration of creation, where all divisions and brokenness are mended. In this vision, God's redemptive work extends beyond individual salvation to encompass the healing of the entire world. The Tree of Life thus becomes a symbol of peace, reconciliation, and wholeness for all people. The nations that once experienced division and suffering are now united in God's kingdom, experiencing the fullness of His healing power.

3. The Tree of Life as a Symbol of Ultimate Redemption:

- Reversal of the Curse: The presence of the Tree of Life in the new Jerusalem signals the complete reversal of the curse that fell upon humanity and creation in Genesis 3. After Adam and Eve's disobedience, they were barred from the Tree of Life, and the ground was cursed (Genesis 3:17-19). In Revelation 22:3, the text explicitly states that "no longer will there be any curse," indicating that the effects of sin and death have been undone. The return of the Tree of Life symbolizes the restoration of creation to its original state of harmony with God.

- Victory Over Death: The Tree of Life is also a powerful symbol of victory over death. In the new Jerusalem, death and suffering no longer exist (Revelation 21:4). The Tree of Life, which grants eternal life, stands as a testament to Christ's victory over death through His resurrection. In this new reality, God's people will enjoy eternal life, free from the fear of death or decay.

The Tree of Life and the Fulfillment of Biblical Themes

1. From Eden to the New Jerusalem:

- The Bookend of Scripture: The Tree of Life serves as a bookend in the biblical narrative, appearing in both the opening chapters of Genesis and the closing chapters of Revelation. In Genesis, the Tree of Life represented God's provision of eternal life for humanity, but access to it was lost due to sin. In Revelation, access to the Tree of Life is restored, symbolizing the completion of God's redemptive work and the fulfillment of His promise to restore creation.

- Paradise Restored: The new Jerusalem represents the ultimate fulfillment of God's plan to restore paradise. What was lost in the fall is now fully restored in the new creation. The Tree of Life, once inaccessible, is now available to all who dwell in the new Jerusalem, representing the restoration of eternal life and communion with God. The vision of the new Jerusalem is not just a return to Eden but an even greater reality where God's presence fills the city, and His people live in perfect harmony with Him.

2. Healing and Reconciliation:

- Healing as a Central Theme: The healing properties of the Tree of Life in Revelation 22:2 highlight the central theme of healing and reconciliation in God's redemptive plan. The nations, often portrayed in the Bible as being at odds with one another, are now healed and united. This reflects the broader biblical vision of God's kingdom, where all peoples and nations are brought together under His reign (Isaiah 2:2-4, Philippians 2:10-11).

- Restoration of Creation: The healing of the nations also extends to the restoration of the created order. The effects of sin, which brought corruption and decay to the natural world, are now reversed. The Tree of Life, a symbol of divine life and healing, signifies that all of creation is being renewed and restored to its original purpose. This healing is comprehensive, encompassing not only humanity but the entire cosmos.

Practical Implications for Believers Today

1. Living in the Hope of Eternal Life:

- The Promise of Eternal Life: Revelation 22:2 offers a powerful reminder of the hope that believers have in Christ. The Tree of Life, which provides continuous sustenance and healing, symbolizes the eternal life that awaits those who remain faithful to God. Believers can live in the assurance that, through Christ, they have access to this eternal life and will one day experience the fullness of God's presence in the new creation.

- Anticipating the New Creation: While the full reality of the new Jerusalem is yet to come, believers are called to live in anticipation of this future. The hope of the new creation should shape how we live in the present, inspiring us to live in faithfulness to God and to participate in His work of healing and reconciliation in the world.

2. Participating in God's Healing Work:

- Agents of Healing and Reconciliation: The imagery of the Tree of Life providing healing for the nations calls believers to be agents of healing and reconciliation in their own communities. Just as the Tree of Life brings healing to the nations in the new creation, believers are called to work for peace, justice, and healing in the present world. This can take many forms, from promoting reconciliation among divided peoples to caring for the environment and working to restore creation.

- Reflecting God's Abundant Life: The Tree of Life represents the abundance of life that comes from God.

As followers of Christ, we are called to reflect this abundant life in our relationships, our work, and our service to others. By living in a way that reflects the values of God's kingdom—love, generosity, peace, and justice—we participate in His work of bringing life and healing to the world.

Revelation 22:2 offers a powerful and hopeful vision of the Tree of Life in the new Jerusalem, symbolizing the fulfillment of God's redemptive plan and the restoration of eternal life for His people. The Tree of Life, with its continuous fruit-bearing and healing properties, represents the abundance of God's provision, the healing of the nations, and the complete reversal of the curse brought about by sin.

For believers today, the promise of the Tree of Life serves as a reminder of the eternal life that awaits in God's presence and the hope of the new creation. It also challenges us to live as agents of healing and reconciliation, participating in God's ongoing work of restoration in the world. As we look forward to the full realization of God's kingdom, we are invited to live in the light of His promises, trusting in His provision and sharing His life-giving presence with others.

Revelation 22:14: The Tree of Life and Its Role in Eternal Life

In the final chapter of the Bible, Revelation 22 provides a powerful conclusion to the biblical story of redemption, restoration, and eternal life. Revelation 22:14 speaks directly to the blessing of those who have access to the Tree of Life, a symbol of eternal life and divine favor:

"Blessed are those who wash their robes, that they may have the right to the tree of life and may go through the gates into the city."

(Revelation 22:14, NIV)

This verse emphasizes the crucial role of the Tree of Life in the believer's ultimate destiny, pointing to the restoration of eternal life and the blessing that comes with access to God's eternal kingdom. The Tree of Life, which once stood in the Garden of Eden but became inaccessible due to sin, is now fully restored in the new Jerusalem, symbolizing the eternal life that is promised to all who follow Christ.

In this chapter, we will explore the significance of the Tree of Life in Revelation 22:14, focusing on its role in granting eternal life, its connection to salvation through Christ, and the implications of this promise for believers.

Context of Revelation 22:14

1. The Closing Vision of Revelation:

- The New Jerusalem: Revelation 22 brings the Bible's grand narrative to its climactic conclusion with a vision of the new Jerusalem. In this eternal city, God's people live in His presence forever, free from sin, suffering, and death. The Tree of Life is central to this vision, representing the restored relationship between God and humanity and the eternal life that comes through God's redemptive plan.

- The Return of the Tree of Life: The Tree of Life, first seen in the Garden of Eden (Genesis 2:9), reappears in Revelation as a symbol of restored access to eternal life. After Adam and Eve sinned, access to the Tree of Life was denied (Genesis 3:22-24), symbolizing the separation from God and the loss of eternal life. Revelation 22 shows the reversal of this separation, as those who have "washed their robes" are granted the right to partake of the Tree of Life and enter the eternal city.

2. Blessed Are Those Who Wash Their Robes:

- Cleansing and Salvation: The phrase "those who wash their robes" refers to those who have been cleansed and made righteous through the blood of Jesus Christ. In Revelation 7:14, a similar phrase is used to describe those who have "washed their robes and made them white in the blood of the Lamb." This metaphor emphasizes the purifying power of Christ's sacrifice, which cleanses believers from sin and makes them worthy to enter God's presence.

- Right to the Tree of Life: The right to access the Tree of Life is granted to those who have been cleansed by Christ's redeeming work. This access signifies the restoration of what was lost in Eden—eternal life and unbroken communion with God. Through Christ, believers are granted the privilege of eternal life, symbolized by the Tree of Life, and are welcomed into the new Jerusalem.

Theological Implications of the Tree of Life in Revelation 22:14

1. The Tree of Life as a Symbol of Eternal Life:

- Restoration of Eternal Life: The Tree of Life in Revelation 22:14 serves as a powerful symbol of the restoration of eternal life. In Genesis, the Tree of Life represented the divine provision of unending life in the presence of God. When Adam and Eve disobeyed God, they were cut off from the Tree of Life, resulting in both physical and spiritual death. In Revelation, however, the curse of sin is undone, and the Tree of Life once again becomes accessible, signifying the full restoration of eternal life.

- Eternal Life Through Christ: The right to the Tree of Life is only granted to those who have been cleansed by Christ's sacrifice. This underscores the theological truth that eternal life is a gift of God's grace, made possible through Jesus' death and resurrection. The Tree of Life, therefore, is not just a symbol of life in the new creation but also a testament to the victory of Christ over sin and death, which makes eternal life possible for all who believe.

2. Access to the Tree of Life and Entrance into the City:

- Entrance Into the Eternal Kingdom: Revelation 22:14 connects the right to the Tree of Life with the privilege of entering the gates of the new Jerusalem. This imagery highlights the intimate relationship between eternal life and entrance into God's eternal kingdom. To have access to the Tree of Life is to be welcomed into the fullness of life in God's presence. The gates of the city are open to those who have been redeemed, and they are free to enjoy the blessings of the new creation.

- The Reversal of the Fall: In Genesis 3, Adam and Eve were driven out of Eden and barred from the Tree of Life, symbolizing their exile from God's presence. In Revelation 22:14, the faithful are welcomed back into the eternal city, and the way to the Tree of Life is opened. This marks the full reversal of the effects of the fall. Where once there was separation and exile, there is now restoration and reunion with God in His eternal kingdom.

3. The Role of the Tree of Life in God's Redemptive Plan:

- The Fulfillment of God's Promise: The presence of the Tree of Life in Revelation 22:14 is the fulfillment of God's promise to restore all things through Christ. Throughout the Bible, the Tree of Life serves as a symbol of God's intention to give eternal life to His people. Its reappearance in Revelation marks the culmination of God's redemptive work, where His people are granted eternal life and the fullness of His blessing.

- A New Creation Reality: The Tree of Life in the new Jerusalem represents the reality of the new creation, where death, suffering, and sin have been eliminated. In this new reality, God's people will live forever in perfect harmony with Him, enjoying the life and abundance that flow from His presence. The Tree of Life stands as a symbol of this new creation, where God's purposes are fully realized, and His people are restored to their intended relationship with Him.

The Tree of Life and the Broader Biblical Narrative

1. The Tree of Life from Genesis to Revelation:

- From Eden to the New Jerusalem: The Tree of Life serves as a bookend to the biblical story, appearing in both the Garden of Eden (Genesis 2:9) and the new Jerusalem (Revelation 22:2, 14). In Eden, the Tree of Life represented God's provision of eternal life, but sin resulted in humanity's separation from the tree. The reappearance of the Tree of Life in Revelation signifies the completion of God's redemptive plan, where eternal life is fully restored.

- Paradise Restored: The promise of access to the Tree of Life in Revelation 22:14 reflects the restoration of paradise. What was lost in Eden—intimacy with God, eternal life, and the blessing of living in God's presence—is now restored in the new creation. The Tree of Life represents the fulfillment of God's plan to bring His people back into perfect fellowship with Him, where they will enjoy eternal life in paradise.

2. Eternal Life as the Ultimate Gift of Redemption:

- Life Through Christ: The Tree of Life in Revelation emphasizes that eternal life is the ultimate gift of redemption, made possible through the life, death, and resurrection of Jesus Christ. Just as the Tree of Life in Eden represented God's life-giving presence, the Tree of Life in the new Jerusalem symbolizes the eternal life that flows from Christ's victory over sin and death. Believers who are washed by the blood of Christ are granted the right to partake of this eternal life, signifying their place in God's kingdom forever.

- Participation in God's Kingdom: Access to the Tree of Life is not just about eternal life in the abstract—it is about participation in the fullness of God's kingdom. To eat from the Tree of Life is to share in the abundant life of the new creation, where God reigns as King, and His people dwell in His presence. The Tree of Life symbolizes the fullness of life that believers will enjoy in the new creation, where they are fully restored and made whole.

Practical Implications for Believers Today

1. The Assurance of Eternal Life:

- Hope in the Promise of Eternal Life: Revelation 22:14 offers a powerful assurance of the promise of eternal life to all who trust in Christ. The right to the Tree of Life is given to those who have been cleansed by the blood of Christ, providing believers with the certainty that they will one day enjoy eternal life in God's presence. This hope sustains believers in the present, giving them the confidence to live faithfully, knowing that their future is secure in Christ.

- Living in Light of the New Creation: While the full reality of the new Jerusalem is yet to come, believers are called to live in anticipation of this future reality. The promise of eternal life should shape how we live in the present, motivating us to live in faithfulness to Christ and to participate in God's work of redemption in the world. The hope of the Tree of Life calls believers to live in a way that reflects the values of God's kingdom, even now.

2. The Call to Purity and Faithfulness:

- Washing Our Robes: Revelation 22:14 emphasizes the importance of being cleansed and purified through Christ. The call to "wash our robes" is a reminder that access to the Tree of Life is only possible through the redemptive work of Christ. Believers are called to continually live in the purity and righteousness that comes through faith in Christ, allowing His grace to transform their lives and prepare them for eternity with God.

- Perseverance in Faith: The promise of eternal life is given to those who persevere in their faith. Revelation consistently calls believers to endure through trials, remain faithful to Christ, and overcome the challenges of this world. The hope of the Tree of Life serves as an encouragement for believers to persevere, knowing that their faithfulness will be rewarded with the gift of eternal life in God's presence.

Revelation 22:14 offers a powerful and hopeful vision of the Tree of Life as the ultimate symbol of eternal life and the culmination of God's redemptive plan. The Tree of Life, which was once lost to humanity due to sin, is now restored through the victory of Christ, who offers eternal life to all who are washed in His blood. The right to eat from the Tree of Life and enter the gates of the new Jerusalem represents the fulfillment of God's promise to restore His people to eternal life and communion with Him.

For believers today, the Tree of Life serves as both a future hope and a present reality. It reminds us that eternal life is available through Christ and that we are called to live in faithfulness, purity, and perseverance. As we look forward to the fullness of life in God's eternal kingdom, we are invited to live in the light of His promises, trusting in His provision and sharing in the abundant life that He offers.

CHAPTER 05

SYMBOLISM AND THEOLOGICAL INSIGHTS

Eternal Life: The Tree of Life as a Symbol of Eternal Life and Divine Favor

The Tree of Life, woven throughout the fabric of Scripture, stands as a profound symbol of eternal life and divine favor. From its first appearance in the Garden of Eden to its climactic return in the book of Revelation, the Tree of Life consistently represents God's desire for humanity to experience eternal communion with Him. It is a symbol of life in its fullness, both physical and spiritual, and reflects God's grace, abundance, and blessing upon His people.

The Tree of Life in the Garden of Eden

1. Symbol of Divine Provision and Eternal Life:

- The Garden of Eden: In Genesis 2:9, the Tree of Life is introduced as part of the paradise that God created for humanity. The Garden of Eden represents a place of perfect harmony between God, humanity, and creation, where Adam and Eve lived in direct communion with God. The Tree of Life was placed in the center of the garden, symbolizing God's provision of eternal life for humanity. It was a sign of God's intention that human beings would live in His presence forever, sustained by His life-giving power.

- Divine Favor and Abundance: The Tree of Life in Eden also represents God's abundant favor toward humanity. Its presence in the garden signifies that God not only created humanity to live but to thrive in a state of perfect blessing and peace. The tree's life-giving properties reflect God's generosity and desire to share His life with His creation, underscoring the idea that eternal life is both a gift and a reflection of God's favor.

2. The Loss of Access to the Tree of Life:

- The Fall and Separation from God: The pivotal moment in Genesis 3, where Adam and Eve disobey God's command and eat from the Tree of the Knowledge of Good and Evil, results in their separation from the Tree of Life. As a consequence of their sin, they are expelled from Eden, and access to the Tree of Life is barred. God's placing of cherubim and a flaming sword to guard the way to the tree (Genesis 3:24) symbolizes the profound separation that sin causes between humanity and eternal life in God's presence.

- Theological Insight—Sin and Mortality: The loss of access to the Tree of Life introduces the concept of mortality into the human experience. Adam and Eve's exile from Eden symbolizes the loss of eternal life and the beginning of physical death. Theologically, this event represents the separation between humanity and God's divine favor, illustrating that sin leads to both spiritual and physical death. The Tree of Life becomes a reminder of what was lost—eternal life with God.

The Tree of Life as a Symbol of Eternal Life

1. Eternal Life in Biblical Theology:

- Life Beyond Mortality: The Tree of Life is a powerful symbol of eternal life, transcending the physical limitations of mortality. Throughout the Bible, eternal life is understood as life that comes from God and is characterized by a relationship with Him. The Tree of Life, therefore, is not just a symbol of unending physical existence but of a life that is full, abundant, and marked by communion with God. This is why access to the Tree of Life is such a central theme in the biblical narrative—it represents the possibility of sharing in God's eternal nature.

- Jesus Christ as the Fulfillment of the Tree of Life: In Christian theology, Jesus Christ is seen as the ultimate fulfillment of the Tree of Life. He refers to Himself as "the resurrection and the life" (John 11:25), and through His death and resurrection, He restores what was lost in Eden. Through faith in Christ, believers are granted access to eternal life, symbolized by the restoration of the Tree of Life in the new Jerusalem (Revelation 22:2). Jesus' offer of eternal life to all who believe in Him is the ultimate expression of divine favor and the fulfillment of God's redemptive plan.

2. Restored Access to Eternal Life in Revelation:

- The Tree of Life in the New Jerusalem: The Tree of Life reappears in Revelation 22, where it stands on either side of the river of the water of life, bearing fruit and providing healing for the nations. In this final vision, the Tree of Life symbolizes the complete restoration of eternal life for those who have been redeemed by Christ. The imagery of the tree's abundant fruit and healing leaves signifies that eternal life in the new creation is marked by complete wholeness, peace, and unending communion with God.

- Theological Insight—Eternal Life as Restored Fellowship: The return of the Tree of Life in Revelation points to the restoration of humanity's relationship with God. In the new Jerusalem, the barriers that sin once created are fully removed, and God's people are invited to eat from the Tree of Life, symbolizing their full participation in God's eternal life. This restored access signifies that God's redemptive plan is complete, and eternal life is not just endless existence but a state of perfect fellowship with God, free from death, pain, or suffering.

The Tree of Life as a Symbol of Divine Favor

1. God's Abundant Provision:

- Divine Favor in the Old Testament: In the Old Testament, the Tree of Life also appears metaphorically, particularly in the wisdom literature. For example, in Proverbs 3:18, wisdom is described as "a tree of life to those who take hold of her." Here, the Tree of Life symbolizes divine favor in the form of wisdom, righteousness, and the pursuit of God's ways. It reflects the idea that living in alignment with

God's will brings life, peace, and blessing—signs of God's favor toward His people.

- The Healing of the Nations: Revelation 22:2 describes the leaves of the Tree of Life as being "for the healing of the nations," signifying the universal nature of God's blessing. The Tree of Life, as a symbol of divine favor, extends not just to individuals but to all of creation. The healing leaves reflect God's plan to restore everything that has been broken by sin, including the divisions between nations. This vision underscores that God's favor is not limited but abundant, bringing restoration and peace to all who are part of His kingdom.

2. The Favor of Access to the Tree of Life:

- Blessing for the Redeemed: Revelation 22:14 promises that those who "wash their robes" will have the right to the Tree of Life. This access is a sign of divine favor and blessing, granted to those who have been cleansed by the blood of Christ. To partake of the Tree of Life is to experience the fullness of God's grace, where eternal life and divine favor are given as gifts to those who are faithful. The Tree of Life, in this context, represents the ultimate blessing—eternal life in God's presence.

- Theological Insight—Divine Favor as Grace: The access to the Tree of Life is a result of God's grace, not human effort. Theologically, this points to the fact that eternal life and divine favor are gifts that come through God's mercy and love, made possible through Christ's atoning work. The Tree of Life serves as a symbol of this grace, reminding believers that eternal life is not earned but freely given to those who trust in Christ.

The Tree of Life and the Hope of Eternal Life

1. Eternal Life as the Fulfillment of God's Promise:

- The Promise of Eternal Life: Throughout Scripture, eternal life is presented as the ultimate hope and promise for God's people. The Tree of Life symbolizes the fulfillment of this promise, offering a vision of the future where believers will experience unending life in God's presence. This hope of eternal life shapes how believers live in the present, as they look forward to the day when they will fully partake of the Tree of Life in the new creation.

- The Joy of Eternal Life: The Tree of Life represents not only life without end but life in its fullest and most joyful sense. In the new Jerusalem, where the Tree of Life flourishes, there is no more death, mourning, crying, or pain (Revelation 21:4). The promise of eternal life is also a promise of eternal joy, where God's people will live in a state of perfect peace and happiness. The Tree of Life, therefore, symbolizes the ultimate fulfillment of human longing for life, joy, and communion with God.

2. Living in Anticipation of Eternal Life:

- Faithfulness and Perseverance: The promise of the Tree of Life in Revelation is given to those who "overcome" (Revelation 2:7) and remain faithful to Christ. This reflects the idea that eternal life is not just a future reality but also something that believers are called to live in anticipation of. The hope of the Tree of Life motivates believers to persevere in their faith, knowing that their reward is the eternal life that comes through Christ.

- Sharing in God's Life Now: While the fullness of eternal life will only be experienced in the new creation, believers are invited to share in God's life even now. Through the indwelling of the Holy Spirit, believers experience a foretaste of eternal life as they live in relationship with God. The Tree of Life, therefore, symbolizes both a present reality—life in Christ—and a future hope, where eternal life will be experienced in all its fullness.

The Tree of Life serves as a powerful and enduring symbol of eternal life and divine favor throughout Scripture. From its first appearance in Eden to its return in the new Jerusalem, the Tree of Life represents God's desire for humanity to share in His eternal life, reflecting His abundant provision, grace, and blessing. The loss of access to the Tree of Life due to sin introduces the theme of separation from God, while its restoration in Revelation signifies the completion of God's redemptive plan and the fulfillment of His promise to grant eternal life to His people.

For believers today, the Tree of Life offers both a present hope and a future reality. It reminds us of the eternal life that is available through Christ and calls us to live in anticipation of the day when we will fully partake of God's eternal life and favor in His kingdom. As we await the fulfillment of this promise, we are invited to experience God's life and grace now, sharing in the blessings of the Tree of Life and looking forward to the joy of eternal communion with Him.

Healing and Restoration

Healing and Restoration: The Tree of Life as a Symbol of Healing for the Nations

The Tree of Life stands as one of the most powerful and hopeful symbols in the Bible, representing not only eternal life but also the healing and restoration of the entire world. In Revelation, the Tree of Life is described as having leaves that are "for the healing of the nations" (Revelation 22:2). This depiction suggests that the redemptive work of God, accomplished through Christ, extends beyond the personal salvation of individuals to the healing and restoration of all creation. The image of the Tree of Life in the New Jerusalem encapsulates the hope of a future where God's peace, justice, and healing are fully realized for all nations.

In this chapter, we will explore the Tree of Life as a symbol of healing and restoration, focusing on its significance for the nations, its role in God's redemptive plan, and the theological implications for believers today.

The Tree of Life in the New Jerusalem

1. The Vision of the New Jerusalem:

- The Healing Tree: Revelation 22:2 presents the Tree of Life in the context of the New Jerusalem, the eternal city of God, where His people will dwell forever. In this vision, the Tree of Life stands on either side of the river of the water of life, symbolizing the abundant and ongoing provision of God's grace and life. Its leaves are said to be "for the healing of the nations," signifying that the redemptive work of God brings not only individual salvation but also global restoration and peace.

- Universal Healing: The phrase "healing of the nations" points to a broader and more comprehensive vision of healing than mere physical restoration. It speaks to the reconciliation of humanity—healing the divisions between nations, cultures, and peoples that have been fractured by sin, strife, and injustice. The Tree of Life represents God's promise to restore all that has been broken by sin, bringing wholeness, peace, and unity to the world.

2. Restoring What Was Broken:

- The Fall and Its Consequences: The introduction of sin into the world in Genesis 3 brought not only death and suffering but also division and enmity between individuals and nations. The curses that came with the fall disrupted relationships between humanity and God, between people, and between humanity and the earth. The loss of access to the Tree of Life after the fall symbolized humanity's separation from God's sustaining life and healing power.

- The Return of the Tree of Life: The reappearance of the Tree of Life in Revelation represents the ultimate reversal of the effects of the fall. In the New Jerusalem, the healing power of the Tree of Life is made available to all, signifying the complete restoration of what was lost in Eden. No longer is humanity barred from the tree; instead, its leaves bring healing to the nations, undoing the damage caused by sin and restoring relationships between people and between nations.

The Healing of the Nations

1. Healing in the Biblical Narrative:

- God's Healing Work Throughout History: The theme of healing runs throughout the Bible, reflecting God's desire to restore both individuals and nations. In the Old Testament, God often promises healing to His people as part of His covenant blessings (e.g., Exodus 15:26, Isaiah 53:5). This healing is not only physical but also spiritual, involving the restoration of broken relationships and the reconciliation of Israel to God.

- Jesus as the Healer: In the New Testament, Jesus' ministry is marked by acts of healing. He heals physical ailments, casts out demons, and restores people to wholeness.

These acts are signs of the in-breaking of the kingdom of God, where healing and restoration are key components of God's redemptive work. Jesus' healings point forward to the ultimate healing that will come in the new creation, where the effects of sin and death will be completely eradicated.

2. Theological Significance of Healing for the Nations:

- Reconciliation Between Nations: The healing of the nations in Revelation 22:2 suggests that the Tree of Life plays a central role in the reconciliation of the divisions and conflicts that have plagued human history. Throughout Scripture, nations are often depicted in opposition to one another, marked by violence, war, and injustice. The healing brought by the Tree of Life signifies the restoration of peace and unity among the nations, as God's redemptive work brings an end to enmity and strife.

- Restoration of Creation: The healing offered by the Tree of Life extends beyond just humanity to encompass all of creation. The fall introduced decay and corruption into the natural world, but Revelation 22:2 points to the renewal of all things. The healing of the nations signifies the restoration of the earth and its ecosystems, as well as the healing of human society. This reflects the broader biblical theme of creation being liberated from the bondage of decay (Romans 8:19-21).

The Role of the Tree of Life in God's Redemptive Plan

1. The Tree of Life and Christ's Redemptive Work:

- Christ as the Source of Healing: The Tree of Life in the new creation is intricately connected to the redemptive work of Christ. Through His life, death, and resurrection, Jesus has secured the healing of humanity and all of creation. Isaiah 53:5 describes the suffering of Christ, saying, "by His wounds we are healed." This healing is comprehensive, covering not only the forgiveness of sins but also the restoration of everything broken by sin. The Tree of Life, as a symbol of eternal life and healing, reflects the fullness of Christ's redemptive power.

- The Leaves for Healing: The leaves of the Tree of Life in Revelation 22:2 are described as having healing properties. This image reflects the healing power of Christ's work, which extends to all aspects of life. Just as the leaves bring healing to the nations, so too does Christ's sacrifice bring healing to the deep wounds caused by sin—both individually and collectively. The Tree of Life symbolizes the life-giving and restorative work of Christ, which heals not only physical and spiritual wounds but also societal and relational divisions.

2. The Final Fulfillment of God's Redemptive Plan:

- A Vision of Cosmic Healing: The Tree of Life in Revelation represents the final fulfillment of God's redemptive plan. It stands as a symbol of the complete restoration that God has promised—a restoration that encompasses all of creation, including humanity, the nations, and the earth itself. The vision of the Tree of Life and the healing of the nations signifies that God's ultimate goal is not only to save individuals but to bring healing and wholeness to the entire cosmos.

- Theological Insight—Restoration of Shalom: The concept of "shalom" in the Bible goes beyond the idea of peace; it refers to wholeness, completeness, and the flourishing of all creation under God's rule. The Tree of Life symbolizes the restoration of shalom, where all things are brought into right relationship with God and with one another. The healing of the nations represents the establishment of God's perfect order, where justice, peace, and harmony prevail.

Practical Implications for Believers Today

1. Participating in God's Healing Work:

- Agents of Healing and Reconciliation: Believers are called to participate in God's work of healing and restoration in the world today. Just as the Tree of Life provides healing for the nations, Christians are called to be agents of reconciliation and peace, working to heal divisions and promote justice. This involves not only sharing the gospel but also engaging in acts of mercy, compassion, and advocacy for the oppressed.

- Promoting Unity and Justice: The vision of the Tree of Life healing the nations challenges believers to work for unity across racial, ethnic, and national lines. The divisions that exist between peoples and nations today are a result of sin, but believers are called to reflect the reconciliation that Christ has accomplished. By promoting justice and working for the healing of societal wounds, believers participate in God's redemptive plan for the world.

2. Hope in the Promise of Healing and Restoration:

- Living in Anticipation of God's Restoration: The promise of the Tree of Life in Revelation 22:2 offers hope to believers that God's ultimate plan is to heal and restore all things. While the fullness of this healing will only be realized in the new creation, believers are called to live in anticipation of this reality. This hope gives strength in the face of suffering and injustice, knowing that God will one day make all things new.

- Personal and Communal Healing: The healing power of the Tree of Life also has personal and communal implications. Believers are invited to experience the healing that comes through Christ in their own lives, whether that involves physical healing, emotional restoration, or spiritual renewal. The church, as the body of Christ, is called to be a place where this healing is nurtured and shared, reflecting the healing power of God to the world.

The Tree of Life as depicted in Revelation 22:2 is a profound symbol of God's ultimate healing and restoration for the nations. Its leaves, which bring healing to the world, reflect God's redemptive work through Christ—a work that restores everything broken by sin, including the divisions between nations and the corruption of creation. The Tree of Life offers hope for a future where all will be made whole, and where peace, justice, and unity will prevail.

For believers today, the Tree of Life serves as both a promise and a calling

. It reminds us that God's plan is to heal and restore all things and that we are invited to participate in this work. As we await the fulfillment of God's kingdom, we are called to be agents of healing and reconciliation in the world, reflecting the life-giving power of Christ to a broken and divided world.

Spiritual Nourishment

Spiritual Nourishment: How the Tree of Life Represents Spiritual Sustenance and Wisdom

The Tree of Life in Scripture serves not only as a symbol of eternal life and healing but also as a powerful metaphor for spiritual sustenance and divine wisdom. From its early mention in the Garden of Eden to its reappearance in Revelation, the Tree of Life reflects God's provision of everything necessary for human flourishing—physical, emotional, and spiritual. In wisdom literature, the Tree of Life is closely tied to living a life of righteousness and embracing God's wisdom, indicating that spiritual nourishment comes from aligning one's life with divine truth.

In this chapter, we will explore the Tree of Life as a symbol of spiritual nourishment and wisdom, examining its significance in both the Old and New Testaments. We will also delve into the theological insights it offers about living a life grounded in God's wisdom and the spiritual sustenance He provides.

The Tree of Life in the Garden of Eden

1. A Source of Life and Sustenance:

- The Tree of Life in Eden: In Genesis 2:9, the Tree of Life is planted by God in the Garden of Eden, where Adam and Eve are invited to live in perfect harmony with God and creation. The Tree of Life serves as a symbol of God's provision for their continued well-being, signifying that their life—both physical and spiritual—depends on their connection to God. It represents the idea that God is the ultimate source of all life and that spiritual sustenance comes from living in His presence.

- Sustaining Eternal Life: The Tree of Life is not just a symbol of physical sustenance; it is a sign of eternal life sustained by God. The nourishment that Adam and Eve would have received from the Tree of Life points to the concept that life, in its fullest and most abundant sense, is given and maintained by God. Spiritual nourishment, therefore, is not something humans can achieve on their own but comes from being in a continual relationship with God, who provides life, wisdom, and sustenance.

2. The Loss of Spiritual Nourishment:

- Separation from the Tree of Life: After Adam and Eve disobey God by eating from the Tree of the Knowledge of Good and Evil, they are expelled from Eden and denied access to the Tree of Life (Genesis 3:22-24). This separation symbolizes the loss of spiritual sustenance and the rupture of the relationship between humanity and God. No longer able to partake of the tree's life-giving properties, Adam and Eve's separation from the Tree of Life signifies humanity's alienation from God and the resulting spiritual death.

- Theological Insight—Spiritual Disconnection: The loss of access to the Tree of Life represents the broader concept of spiritual disconnection from God. Without the sustaining presence of God, humanity is left to face the consequences of sin—spiritual emptiness, mortality, and the inability to live in the fullness of life that God intended. This moment in the biblical narrative sets the stage for the need for reconciliation and the restoration of spiritual nourishment through God's redemptive work.

The Tree of Life and Wisdom in the Old Testament

1. The Tree of Life in Wisdom Literature:

- Proverbs 3:18—Wisdom as a Tree of Life: In the book of Proverbs, wisdom is often depicted as a source of life, with Proverbs 3:18 explicitly stating, "She [wisdom] is a tree of life to those who take hold of her; those who hold her fast will be blessed." Here, the Tree of Life is used as a metaphor for the life-giving and sustaining qualities of divine wisdom. Just as the Tree of Life in Eden provided sustenance, so too does wisdom nourish the soul and lead to a flourishing life.

- The Connection Between Wisdom and Spiritual Nourishment: Proverbs teaches that spiritual nourishment comes from living in accordance with God's wisdom. Wisdom, in this context, is more than intellectual knowledge—it is the skillful and righteous application of divine truth in one's life. By following God's wisdom, individuals experience spiritual nourishment, growth, and fulfillment, much like the sustenance that the Tree of Life provided in Eden.

2. Righteousness and Life in the Wisdom Books:

- Proverbs 11:30—The Fruit of Righteousness: Another instance where the Tree of Life is used metaphorically is in Proverbs 11:30, which says, "The fruit of the righteous is a tree of life, and the one who is wise saves lives." This verse links righteousness and wisdom to spiritual nourishment and vitality. Just as the Tree of Life produces fruit that sustains life, so does living righteously and in alignment with God's wisdom bring life and blessings to oneself and others.

- Theological Insight—Wisdom as Spiritual Food: In wisdom literature, the Tree of Life represents more than just physical nourishment; it embodies the idea that true life comes from living wisely and righteously according to God's commands. Spiritual nourishment, then, is the result of embracing divine wisdom, which leads to a flourishing life characterized by peace, joy, and purpose. The Tree of Life in these contexts becomes a symbol of the spiritual sustenance that comes from living in harmony with God's will.

The Tree of Life as Spiritual Sustenance in Revelation

1. Restored Access to the Tree of Life:

- Revelation 22:2—The Tree of Life in the New Jerusalem: The Tree of Life reappears in Revelation 22, where it grows on either side of the river of the water of life in the New Jerusalem. This vision of the restored Tree of Life signifies the full restoration of the relationship between God and humanity, where the spiritual nourishment lost in Eden is fully restored. In the new creation, the Tree of Life bears fruit continuously, providing eternal sustenance to God's people, symbolizing that spiritual nourishment will never be lacking in God's presence.

- Eternal Spiritual Nourishment: The Tree of Life in Revelation represents the unending spiritual sustenance that believers will receive in eternity. It symbolizes the eternal life that flows from God's presence and highlights that spiritual nourishment is not a one-time event but an ongoing experience. In the New Jerusalem, believers will be in perfect communion with God, continually partaking of His wisdom, life, and sustenance.

2. Healing and Spiritual Wholeness:

- Leaves for the Healing of the Nations: Revelation 22:2 also describes the leaves of the Tree of Life as being "for the healing of the nations." This healing imagery reflects not only physical restoration but also spiritual wholeness. In this final vision, the Tree of Life becomes a symbol of God's ultimate plan to restore all things, healing the brokenness caused by sin and providing complete spiritual and physical nourishment for all people.

- Theological Insight—Spiritual Healing and Fulfillment: The Tree of Life's role in providing healing for the nations underscores the idea that spiritual nourishment leads to healing and wholeness. In God's eternal kingdom, there will be no lack of spiritual sustenance, as the Tree of Life offers continual nourishment, healing, and restoration. This healing encompasses not only individuals but entire nations, reflecting the universal scope of God's redemptive work.

The Tree of Life and Spiritual Wisdom in the Life of Believers

1. Spiritual Nourishment Through Christ:

- Christ as the Source of Life: In the New Testament, Jesus identifies Himself as the source of spiritual life and sustenance. In John 6:35, Jesus declares, "I am the bread of life. Whoever comes to me will never go hungry, and whoever believes in me will never be thirsty." This statement echoes the themes associated with the Tree of Life, where Christ is the ultimate source of spiritual nourishment. Just as the Tree of Life provided sustenance in Eden, Jesus provides the spiritual food that sustains believers.

- Abiding in Christ for Spiritual Growth: In John 15:5, Jesus describes Himself as the "vine," and believers are the "branches." By abiding in Him, believers are nourished and empowered to grow spiritually. This connection to Christ as the source of spiritual life reflects the deeper truth that spiritual nourishment comes from remaining in relationship with Him. Through Christ, believers receive the wisdom, strength, and sustenance needed to live a life that honors God.

2. Living a Life of Wisdom and Righteousness:

- The Pursuit of Wisdom: For believers, spiritual nourishment also involves the pursuit of divine wisdom. The Tree of Life in Proverbs serves as a reminder that living in accordance with God's wisdom brings spiritual vitality and life. This means seeking God's guidance in daily decisions, studying His Word, and applying biblical principles to life. In doing so, believers experience the spiritual nourishment that comes from walking in God's ways.

- The Role of the Holy Spirit: The Holy Spirit plays a crucial role in providing spiritual nourishment and wisdom to believers. As the Spirit of truth, He guides believers into all truth (John 16:13), offering divine insight and wisdom for living a life that pleases God. The Spirit sustains believers spiritually, much like the Tree of Life, by continually feeding them with wisdom, understanding, and the strength to persevere in their faith.

Practical Implications for Believers Today

1. Seeking Spiritual Nourishment in God's Presence:

- Daily Communion with God: Just as the Tree of Life provided nourishment in Eden, believers are called to seek spiritual sustenance through daily communion with God. This involves spending time in prayer, reading Scripture, and meditating on God's wisdom. By remaining connected to God, believers experience the spiritual growth and nourishment that come from abiding in His presence.

- Embracing God's Wisdom: Spiritual nourishment also comes from embracing God's wisdom and applying it to life. Believers are encouraged to seek wisdom through the study of Scripture, the guidance of the Holy Spirit, and wise counsel from others. Living a life grounded in God's wisdom leads to spiritual flourishing, much like the Tree of Life brings forth fruit in abundance.

2. Sharing Spiritual Nourishment with Others:

- Bearing Fruit for Others: As the Tree of Life bears fruit for the nourishment of others, believers are called to bear spiritual fruit that benefits those around them. This means living in a way that reflects God's love, wisdom, and truth, offering encouragement, support, and spiritual guidance to others. By sharing the spiritual nourishment they receive from God, believers participate in the work of extending God's life-giving presence to the world.

- Promoting Spiritual Wholeness and Healing: Believers are also called to be agents of spiritual healing, reflecting the Tree of Life's role in providing healing for the nations. This involves promoting peace, justice, and reconciliation, as well as offering spiritual care to those in need. Through acts of kindness, prayer, and service, believers can help bring spiritual healing and nourishment to a broken world.

The Tree of Life stands as a profound symbol of spiritual nourishment and wisdom throughout Scripture. From its role in Eden to its restoration in the New Jerusalem, the Tree of Life represents the sustenance that comes from living in relationship with God and embracing His wisdom. For believers today, the Tree of Life points to the importance of seeking spiritual nourishment through Christ, living a life grounded in divine wisdom, and sharing God's life-giving presence with others.

As we partake of the spiritual nourishment that God provides, we are invited to experience the fullness of life that He offers—a life marked by wisdom, growth, and flourishing in His presence.

CHAPTER 06

COMPARATIVE ANALYSIS

Other Biblical Trees: A Comparison with Other Significant Trees in the Bible

The Bible is rich with symbolic references to trees, which often represent life, provision, and divine encounters. Among the many trees mentioned, the Tree of Life stands out as a central symbol of eternal life, spiritual nourishment, and divine wisdom. However, other trees also play significant roles throughout Scripture, each contributing to the theological narrative in unique ways. From the Tree of the Knowledge of Good and Evil to the fig tree, olive tree, and even the cross, these trees offer layers of spiritual meaning, teaching us about human experience, faith, and God's plan for redemption.

In this chapter, we will compare the Tree of Life with other significant biblical trees, exploring their roles, symbolism, and theological significance. By examining these trees side by side, we will gain a deeper understanding of how they contribute to the overarching biblical narrative.

1. The Tree of the Knowledge of Good and Evil

1. Role in the Genesis Narrative:

- The Tree of Life and the Tree of the Knowledge of Good and Evil: In the Garden of Eden, alongside the Tree of Life stands the Tree of the Knowledge of Good and Evil (Genesis 2:9). While the Tree of Life symbolizes eternal life and communion with God, the Tree of the Knowledge of Good and Evil represents the moral choice given to humanity. God commanded Adam and Eve not to eat from this tree, as doing so would lead to spiritual death and the loss of innocence (Genesis 2:16-17).

- Theological Contrast: The Tree of Life is a symbol of God's sustaining grace and the possibility of living forever in His presence, while the Tree of the Knowledge of

Good and Evil represents autonomy, moral responsibility, and the consequences of disobedience. The moment Adam and Eve chose to eat from the forbidden tree, they introduced sin into the world, resulting in their separation from the Tree of Life and the beginning of mortality. Thus, these two trees together represent the choice between obedience to God and the pursuit of self-determination.

2. The Impact of the Fall:

- Loss of Access to the Tree of Life: After Adam and Eve ate from the Tree of the Knowledge of Good and Evil, they were banished from the Garden of Eden and barred from accessing the Tree of Life (Genesis 3:22-24). This event highlights the connection between spiritual death and the loss of eternal life. The Tree of the Knowledge of Good and Evil, therefore, stands as a reminder of the consequences of disobedience, whereas the Tree of Life represents the life-giving relationship with God that was lost but will be restored through redemption.

- Theological Insight—Choice and Consequence: The Tree of the Knowledge of Good and Evil teaches us about the role of human choice in the biblical narrative. It symbolizes free will and the responsibility that comes with it. The Tree of Life, by contrast, offers the assurance of eternal sustenance when humanity is in alignment with God's will. Together, these trees reflect the balance between free will and divine grace in the human experience.

2. The Olive Tree

1. Symbol of Peace and Covenant:

- The Olive Tree in the Flood Narrative: One of the most well-known references to the olive tree is found in the story of Noah's ark. After the flood, a dove returns to Noah with an olive leaf in its beak, signaling the end of God's judgment and the beginning of new life (Genesis 8:11). The olive tree here symbolizes peace, hope, and the renewal of God's covenant with humanity.

- Comparison with the Tree of Life: While the Tree of Life represents eternal life and spiritual nourishment, the olive tree is closely associated with peace, anointing, and covenant renewal. Both trees share themes of life and blessing, but the olive tree's significance lies in its connection to restoration after judgment. In this way, the olive tree can be seen as a precursor to the ultimate renewal of life that the Tree of Life offers in the new creation.

2. Symbol of Israel and God's People:

- Paul's Olive Tree Analogy: In Romans 11, the Apostle Paul uses the olive tree as a metaphor for the people of God. He describes Israel as the natural branches of the olive tree, while Gentile believers are like wild branches grafted into the tree (Romans 11:17-24). This image emphasizes the unity of God's people and His plan of salvation for both Jews and Gentiles.

- Theological Insight—Spiritual Inclusion: The olive tree, like the Tree of Life, represents inclusion in God's covenant community. Just as the Tree of Life offers healing and sustenance to all nations in the new Jerusalem, the olive tree in Paul's analogy highlights the universal nature of God's redemptive plan. Both trees symbolize God's desire to bring all people into a life-giving relationship with Him.

3. The Fig Tree

1. The Fig Tree as a Symbol of Fruitfulness and Judgment:

- The Fruitless Fig Tree: In the Gospels, Jesus curses a barren fig tree, which withers immediately (Matthew 21:18-19). This event serves as a symbol of judgment against fruitlessness, particularly in relation to Israel's failure to bear spiritual fruit. The fig tree often represents fruitfulness and prosperity in the Bible, but its lack of fruit in this instance symbolizes spiritual barrenness and the consequences of failing to live according to God's will.

- Comparison with the Tree of Life: While the Tree of Life is a source of continual fruit and represents eternal life, the fig tree in this narrative symbolizes the opposite—spiritual emptiness and judgment. The withering of the fig tree serves as a warning to those who fail to produce the fruits of righteousness, in contrast to the Tree of Life, which offers eternal sustenance and spiritual vitality to those who are faithful.

2. Fig Leaves in the Garden of Eden:

- Fig Leaves as a Covering: Interestingly, the fig tree plays a role in the Genesis narrative when Adam and Eve use fig leaves to cover themselves after realizing their nakedness (Genesis 3:7). This act symbolizes the attempt to cover shame and guilt after sin. In contrast to the Tree of Life, which provides life and spiritual nourishment, the fig leaves represent a temporary and insufficient solution to the problem of sin.

- Theological Insight—False Security: The use of fig leaves to cover nakedness illustrates humanity's tendency to rely on superficial solutions rather than seeking true healing and restoration from God. The Tree of Life offers the true remedy for sin—eternal life and healing—while the fig tree in this context symbolizes inadequate attempts to address the deeper issue of spiritual separation from God.

4. The Cross (The Tree of Crucifixion)

1. The Cross as the "Tree" of Redemption:

- The Cross as a Tree: In the New Testament, the cross is sometimes referred to as a "tree," particularly in the writings of Peter (Acts 5:30; 1 Peter 2:24). The cross, as the instrument of Christ's crucifixion, becomes a tree of redemption, where Jesus bore the sins of humanity and opened the way to eternal life. The cross, therefore, stands in contrast to the Tree of the Knowledge of Good and Evil, which brought death. Through the "tree" of the cross, Christ's sacrificial death brings life and reconciliation.

- Comparison with the Tree of Life: The cross and the Tree of Life are deeply interconnected symbols. The Tree of Life represents the eternal life made possible by God's grace, while the cross is the means by which that eternal life is secured. Through the cross, the curse of sin is reversed, and access to the Tree of Life is restored. The cross, like the Tree of Life, offers spiritual nourishment and healing, as Christ's sacrifice opens the way for believers to partake of eternal life.

2. Theological Insight—From Death to Life:

- Redemption Through the Cross: The cross, often referred to as a "tree," symbolizes the paradox of life emerging from death. Just as the Tree of Life offers eternal sustenance, the cross provides the way to that life through Christ's death and resurrection. The "tree" of the cross and the Tree of Life are united in their role within God's redemptive plan: one offering salvation through sacrifice, the other offering the fullness of eternal life to those who have been redeemed.

The Tree of Life holds a central place in the biblical narrative, symbolizing eternal life, divine sustenance, and spiritual nourishment. However, other trees in the Bible, such as the Tree of the Knowledge of Good and Evil, the olive tree, the fig tree, and the cross, also carry profound spiritual meaning. Each of these trees adds to the richness of biblical symbolism, offering insights into human experience, sin, redemption, and the nature of God's covenant with His people.

By comparing the Tree of Life with these other significant trees, we can see how they collectively contribute to the overarching themes of life, death, judgment, and salvation. While the Tree of Life represents the ultimate goal of eternal life and restoration, each of the other trees offers unique theological insights into the journey toward that final destination.

This chapter compares the Tree of Life with other significant trees in the Bible, such as the Tree of the Knowledge of Good and Evil, the olive tree, the fig tree, and the cross. Each tree contributes to the biblical narrative in unique ways, offering insights into themes of life, death, redemption, and spiritual nourishment. Through this comparative analysis, we gain a deeper understanding of the role of trees in Scripture and their theological significance in God's redemptive plan.

Cultural Context

How the Concept of the Tree of Life Fits Within the Broader Ancient Near Eastern Context

The Tree of Life, a powerful symbol throughout the Bible, is not an isolated concept within the ancient world. Trees in general, and the concept of a life-giving or sacred tree in particular, held significant meaning in many ancient Near Eastern cultures. The broader cultural context of the Ancient Near East (ANE), which includes Mesopotamia, Egypt, and Canaan, was rich with imagery related to sacred trees, fertility, divine provision, and immortality. Understanding how the biblical Tree of Life fits within this cultural landscape allows for a deeper appreciation of its unique theological significance while recognizing its connection to the broader world in which the Bible was written.

In this chapter, we will explore the symbolism of sacred trees in ancient Near Eastern cultures and compare these with the biblical concept of the Tree of Life. We will analyze the similarities and differences, highlighting the unique ways the Bible uses the Tree of Life to convey theological truths about God, life, and human destiny.

Sacred Trees in the Ancient Near East

1. The Symbolism of Trees in the ANE:

- Trees as Symbols of Life and Fertility: In many ancient Near Eastern cultures, trees were symbols of life, fertility, and sustenance. Trees, with their roots in the earth and branches reaching toward the heavens, were often seen as mediators between the divine and the human realms. They were frequently associated with divine blessing, agricultural fertility, and the cycles of life, death, and renewal. The evergreen tree, in particular, often symbolized immortality and eternal life, as its leaves remained green throughout the year.

- The Mesopotamian Tree of Life: In Mesopotamian mythology, sacred trees played a prominent role, often connected with divine realms and immortality. For example, in the Epic of Gilgamesh, one of the oldest recorded pieces of literature, the hero Gilgamesh seeks out a sacred plant that is said to offer eternal life. Similarly, other Mesopotamian art and literature frequently depict a "tree of life" motif, often guarded by divine beings or situated in sacred gardens. These trees were considered symbols of divine wisdom, power, and the life-giving nature of the gods.

2. Trees and Divine Kingship:

- The Tree as a Symbol of Kingship: In many ancient Near Eastern cultures, trees were also associated with kingship and divine authority. For instance, in Assyrian art, the tree of life was often depicted alongside the king, symbolizing the monarch's connection to the divine and his role as the mediator between heaven and earth. The tree represented both the king's authority to rule and his ability to ensure the fertility and prosperity of the land.

- The Egyptian Tree of Life: In ancient Egypt, sacred trees were also connected with kingship and the afterlife. The sycamore tree, in particular, was believed to be the tree of life, offering sustenance and immortality to the dead. In Egyptian mythology, the goddess Hathor was often depicted as a tree deity, offering nourishment to the souls of the deceased from the branches of the sycamore. This concept of a life-giving tree associated with immortality and the afterlife parallels the biblical Tree of Life, though the context and theological meaning differ.

Comparing the Tree of Life with ANE Sacred Trees

1. Similarities Between the Tree of Life and ANE Sacred Trees:

- Life and Fertility: Like the sacred trees of the ancient Near East, the biblical Tree of Life represents life, fertility, and sustenance. Both the biblical and ANE trees are often associated with divine provision and the blessings of abundance, reflecting the importance of agriculture and the cycles of nature in ancient societies.

- Immortality and Eternal Life: The concept of a tree that grants eternal life is a recurring theme in many ancient Near Eastern cultures, including Mesopotamia and Egypt. The Tree of Life in the Bible shares this characteristic, as it offers the possibility of eternal life to Adam and Eve in the Garden of Eden. This similarity suggests that the biblical writers were familiar with these widespread motifs, but they adapted and transformed them within the framework of Israel's theology.

- Gardens as Sacred Spaces: Both in the Bible and in other ANE cultures, sacred trees are often located in gardens or divine realms. The Garden of Eden in Genesis 2-3, where the Tree of Life is located, parallels the sacred gardens found in Mesopotamian and Canaanite mythology, where gods dwelled and life-giving trees grew. These gardens were seen as places of divine encounter and blessing, reinforcing the idea that the Tree of Life is part of a sacred space where humanity can experience communion with God.

2. Differences in Theological Emphasis:

- Monotheism vs. Polytheism: One of the most significant differences between the biblical Tree of Life and the sacred trees of the ancient Near East is the theological framework in which they are situated. In ANE cultures, sacred trees were often associated with a pantheon of gods, each responsible for different aspects of life, such as fertility, kingship, or the afterlife. In contrast, the biblical Tree of Life is firmly rooted in Israel's monotheistic belief in Yahweh as the one true God, who alone gives life and sustains creation. The Tree of Life is a direct symbol of God's provision and grace, rather than being linked to multiple deities.

- Theological Role of Humanity: In the ANE context, the sacred trees often reinforced the idea of kingship and the divine right of rulers, who mediated between the gods and the people. The biblical Tree of Life, however, is accessible to all of humanity, not just the elite or the king. In the Garden of Eden, Adam and Eve are invited to partake of the Tree of Life, signifying that eternal life and communion with God are meant for all people, not just a select few. This reflects the biblical theme of humanity's special relationship with God and the universal offer of life and blessing.

The Tree of Life in Israel's Theology

1. Yahweh as the Source of Life:

- The Tree of Life and Divine Provision: Unlike the sacred trees of ANE mythology, which were often connected to fertility deities or gods of vegetation, the Tree of Life in the

Bible is a direct symbol of Yahweh's provision. In Israel's theology, God alone is the giver of life, and the Tree of Life represents His desire for humanity to share in His eternal life. This connection emphasizes that life, both physical and spiritual, is a gift from God, and the Tree of Life serves as a reminder of humanity's dependence on God for sustenance and well-being.

- God's Sovereignty Over Creation: The Tree of Life is also a symbol of God's sovereignty over creation. While the ANE sacred trees were often part of a pantheon of gods who were believed to control different aspects of nature, the Bible presents Yahweh as the Creator of all things, including the Tree of Life. This reflects a theological shift in the understanding of sacred trees: rather than being objects of veneration or representations of deities, the Tree of Life points to the one true God who is Lord over all creation.

2. Wisdom and Life in Israel's Theology:

- The Tree of Life and Wisdom: Another unique aspect of the Tree of Life in Israel's theology is its association with wisdom. In Proverbs, wisdom is described as a "tree of life" to those who embrace it (Proverbs 3:18). This metaphor emphasizes that living according to God's wisdom leads to a flourishing, abundant life, much like the Tree of Life in the

Garden of Eden offered sustenance and vitality. This wisdom tradition reflects Israel's belief that true life comes from aligning one's life with God's will, in contrast to the ANE focus on divine favor through rituals or kingship.

- The Promise of Restoration: The Tree of Life also plays a role in Israel's eschatological hope for the future. While access to the Tree of Life was lost in the Garden of Eden due to sin, the Bible holds out the promise of restoration. In the book of Revelation, the Tree of Life reappears in the new Jerusalem, where it provides healing and eternal life for all who are redeemed (Revelation 22:2). This reflects Israel's hope for the ultimate restoration of creation, where humanity will once again enjoy unbroken fellowship with God.

The Tree of Life and Its Unique Theological Contribution

1. Redemption and Restoration:

- The Fall and Redemption Narrative: The Tree of Life plays a central role in the biblical narrative of creation, fall, and redemption. While sacred trees in the ANE often functioned as symbols of divine blessing or kingship, the Tree of Life in the Bible is deeply connected to humanity's moral and spiritual journey. Its presence in Eden before the fall represents God's intention for humanity to live in eternal communion with Him, while its reappearance in Revelation symbolizes the fulfillment of God's redemptive plan.

- A Theology of Hope: The Bible presents the Tree of Life not only as a symbol of life and provision but also as a symbol of hope. In contrast to ANE myths that often depicted a cyclical view of life, death, and renewal, the biblical narrative presents a linear progression from creation to redemption. The Tree of Life points to the ultimate restoration of all things, where God's people will enjoy eternal life in His presence. This eschatological hope sets the biblical Tree of Life apart from its counterparts in other ancient cultures, emphasizing God's redemptive purposes for all of humanity.

2. Universal Access to Life:

- God's Invitation to All: While sacred trees in the ANE were often reserved for kings or the elite, the Bible presents the Tree of Life as a symbol of God's universal invitation to life. In both the Garden of Eden and the new Jerusalem, the Tree of Life is available to all who are in right relationship with God. This reflects the biblical theme of inclusivity, where God's blessings are extended to all nations and peoples who seek Him. In Revelation 22:2, the leaves of the Tree of Life are described as being "for the healing of the nations," underscoring the universal scope of God's redemptive plan.

The concept of the Tree of Life in the Bible shares significant commonalities with sacred trees in the broader ancient Near Eastern context, such as representing life, fertility, and divine provision. However, the Tree of Life stands out in Israel's theology for its unique role in the story of creation, fall, and redemption. While sacred trees in other cultures were often tied to fertility gods, kingship, or rituals, the Tree of Life in Scripture serves as a profound symbol of God's grace, wisdom, and eternal life.

By examining the Tree of Life in its cultural context, we gain a deeper appreciation for its distinct theological contribution to the biblical narrative. It symbolizes not only the life that God offers but also the hope of restoration, where humanity will one day regain access to the Tree of Life and live in eternal communion with God.

This chapter explores the cultural context of the Tree of Life, comparing it with other significant trees in the ancient Near Eastern world. While similarities exist in themes of life, fertility, and immortality, the biblical Tree of Life offers a unique theological perspective on eternal life, redemption, and the universal scope of God's invitation to humanity.

Theological Reflection

Implications for Understanding God's Plan of Redemption and Restoration

The Tree of Life, from its first mention in the Garden of Eden to its reappearance in the New Jerusalem, serves as a profound symbol of God's overarching plan for redemption and restoration. Its presence throughout the biblical narrative signifies the connection between creation, fall, redemption, and ultimate restoration, pointing to God's desire to bring humanity back into eternal fellowship with Him. In this chapter, we will reflect on the theological implications of the Tree of Life, exploring how it illuminates key aspects of God's redemptive plan, including eternal life, reconciliation, and the hope of a restored creation.

The Tree of Life and Creation

1. God's Original Intention for Humanity:

- A Symbol of Eternal Life: In the Garden of Eden, the Tree of Life represents God's intention for humanity to enjoy eternal life in His presence. Adam and Eve were created to live in unbroken fellowship with God, and the Tree of Life symbolized the life-sustaining power that flows from this relationship. This eternal life was not just physical but also spiritual, reflecting the wholeness and peace (shalom) that comes from being in harmony with the Creator.

- Life and Divine Provision: The presence of the Tree of Life in the center of Eden underscores that life itself is a gift from God, dependent on His provision. Humanity was intended to partake of the tree's fruit, living in continual reliance on God's sustenance. Theologically, this points to the idea that true life—both physical and spiritual—cannot be separated from God, who is the source of all life.

2. The Loss of Life Through Sin:

- The Fall and Separation from God: The act of disobedience in eating from the Tree of the Knowledge of Good and Evil led to humanity's separation from God and loss of access to the Tree of Life (Genesis 3:22-24). This moment marks the introduction of sin and death into the human experience, highlighting the consequences of choosing autonomy over dependence on God. Theologically, this separation from the Tree of Life symbolizes spiritual death—a disconnection from the life and sustenance that comes from God alone.

- The Need for Redemption: The expulsion from Eden and the barred access to the Tree of Life emphasize humanity's need for redemption. Without access to the Tree of Life, humanity faces death and separation from God, but the biblical narrative promises that this condition is not permanent. The loss of access to the Tree of Life sets the stage for the rest of Scripture, which unfolds God's plan to restore humanity to eternal life and fellowship with Him.

The Tree of Life and Redemption

1. The Cross as the Pathway to Life:

- The Cross and the Tree of Life: Theologically, the Tree of Life is closely connected to the cross of Christ. While the Tree of Life offers eternal life, humanity's sin has barred access to it. Jesus, through His sacrificial death on the cross, makes it possible for humanity to regain access to eternal life. The cross is sometimes referred to as a "tree" in the New Testament (Acts 5:30, Galatians 3:13), linking it symbolically to the Tree of Life. Just as Adam and Eve lost access to the Tree of Life through disobedience, Christ's obedience unto death opens the way for believers to partake of eternal life once again.

- Reversing the Curse: The cross represents the reversal of the curse that came with humanity's sin in Eden. In Galatians 3:13, Paul writes that "Christ redeemed us from the curse of the law by becoming a curse for us," referring to the curse of death that sin brought into the world. By taking on this curse, Jesus restores what was lost, including the possibility of eternal life in God's presence. The Tree of Life, which was once inaccessible due to sin, becomes available again through the redemptive work of Christ.

2. The Promise of New Life:

- Eternal Life Through Christ: Jesus often speaks of eternal life as the central gift of salvation. In John 10:28, He promises, "I give them eternal life, and they shall never perish." This echoes the promise of the Tree of Life in the Garden of Eden and its ultimate fulfillment in the New Jerusalem. Eternal life is more than just living forever—it is a restored relationship with God, where believers experience the fullness of life that comes from being in His presence.

- Spiritual Sustenance and Rebirth: The Tree of Life, much like Christ Himself, represents ongoing spiritual sustenance. Just as the Tree of Life in the Garden of Eden was a continual source of nourishment, Christ offers continual spiritual sustenance to those who believe in Him.

Through the Holy Spirit, believers experience a new birth, marked by a restored relationship with God and the indwelling presence of His life-giving Spirit (John 3:5-6). Theologically, this points to the idea that eternal life begins not in the distant future but in the present for those who are in Christ.

The Tree of Life and Restoration

1. The Restoration of Creation:

- The Tree of Life in the New Jerusalem: Revelation 22 describes the reappearance of the Tree of Life in the new Jerusalem, signaling the restoration of what was lost in Eden. In this final vision, the Tree of Life stands on either side of the river of the water of life, bearing fruit every month, and its leaves are "for the healing of the nations" (Revelation 22:2). This imagery reflects the full restoration of God's original intention for creation, where humanity and all of creation are healed and brought back into harmony with God.

- Healing of the Nations: The Tree of Life in the new Jerusalem symbolizes not only personal redemption but also the restoration of the entire world. The leaves of the Tree of Life provide healing for the nations, indicating that God's redemptive plan extends beyond individuals to the renewal of all creation. Theologically, this points to the eschatological hope that in the new creation, all divisions, conflicts, and brokenness will be healed. God's plan for restoration includes the reconciliation of peoples and nations, as well as the healing of the earth itself.

2. The Hope of New Creation:

- God's Ultimate Purpose: The reappearance of the Tree of Life in Revelation highlights God's ultimate purpose: to bring humanity back into eternal communion with Him and to restore the entire created order. The Tree of Life in the new Jerusalem represents the completion of God's redemptive plan, where sin, death, and suffering are no more, and humanity once again has access to eternal life. This vision provides believers with the hope that God's purposes will be fully realized in the future, where His kingdom will reign in peace and righteousness forever.

- Eternal Fellowship with God: At the heart of the Tree of Life's symbolism is the promise of eternal fellowship with God. In the new creation, the Tree of Life will stand as a constant reminder of the life and healing that flow from God's presence. Theologically, this emphasizes the restoration of the relationship between God and humanity, where the barriers caused by sin have been removed, and believers are able to live in perfect harmony with God for eternity.

Implications for Believers

1. Living in the Hope of Restoration:

- Eternal Life as a Present and Future Reality: The promise of the Tree of Life challenges believers to live in light of both the present reality of spiritual life in Christ and the future hope of eternal life in God's kingdom. While the fullness of eternal life will be experienced in the new creation, believers are called to live now in a way that reflects the life of the kingdom. This includes experiencing the spiritual sustenance that comes through communion with Christ and living in anticipation of the day when all things will be made new.

- Participation in God's Redemptive Work: Believers are invited to participate in God's redemptive work by living as agents of healing and reconciliation in the world. Just as the Tree of Life offers healing for the nations, Christians are called to promote peace, justice, and restoration in their communities and in the world at large. This reflects the broader theological truth that God's redemption extends to all of creation, and believers are called to be instruments of that redemption.

2. The Call to Faithfulness and Perseverance:

- Overcoming Through Christ: Revelation 2:7 promises, "To the one who is victorious, I will give the right to eat from the tree of life, which is in the paradise of God." This promise serves as both an encouragement and a call to faithfulness. Believers are called to persevere in their faith, knowing that eternal life is the reward for those who overcome the trials and challenges of this world. The Tree of Life symbolizes the hope of eternal life that sustains believers as they follow Christ.

- Spiritual Nourishment in the Present: While the Tree of Life points to a future reality, it also offers a reminder that believers can experience spiritual nourishment in the present through their relationship with Christ. Just as the Tree of Life provided continual sustenance in Eden, Jesus offers believers the spiritual nourishment they need to grow in their faith and live in alignment with God's will. This nourishment comes through the Word of God, prayer, and the indwelling of the Holy Spirit.

The Tree of Life serves as a profound theological symbol that illuminates God's plan of redemption and restoration. From the beginning of creation, where it represents eternal life in the Garden of Eden, to its reappearance in the new Jerusalem, where it signifies the healing of the nations, the Tree of Life encapsulates the overarching narrative of Scripture. It reveals God's desire for humanity to live in eternal fellowship with Him and highlights the hope of restoration through Christ's redemptive work.

For believers, the Tree of Life offers both a present and future reality—spiritual nourishment in this life through Christ and the promise of eternal life in the age to come. It reminds us of God's ultimate purpose to restore all of creation and invites us to live in the hope of that future while participating in His redemptive work in the present.

This chapter reflects on the theological implications of the Tree of Life, exploring how it reveals God's plan of redemption and restoration. The Tree of Life symbolizes eternal life, spiritual sustenance, and the hope of a restored creation, offering believers both a present reality of life in Christ and a future hope of eternal fellowship with God.

CHAPTER 07

PRACTICAL APPLICATIONS

Personal Reflection: How the Symbolism of the Tree of Life Can Impact Personal Spiritual Growth

The Tree of Life, as a symbol of divine provision, eternal life, and spiritual nourishment, has profound implications for personal spiritual growth. Its symbolism speaks to the ongoing process of spiritual transformation, offering believers a deeper understanding of their relationship with God and their journey toward spiritual maturity. By reflecting on the Tree of Life, Christians can find inspiration for their daily walk with God, as it calls them to seek spiritual sustenance, embrace wisdom, and live in the hope of eternal life.

In this chapter, we will explore how the symbolism of the Tree of Life can impact personal spiritual growth, offering practical insights for applying this rich biblical image to the daily life of faith.

1. Spiritual Sustenance from God

1. Dependence on God for Life and Growth:

- God as the Source of Life: The Tree of Life in the Garden of Eden symbolized the life that flowed from God to humanity. In the same way, believers today are called to depend on God for their spiritual life and growth. Recognizing that spiritual nourishment comes from God alone leads to a deeper sense of reliance on Him for strength, wisdom, and guidance.

- Personal Reflection: As we reflect on the Tree of Life, we are reminded to stay connected to the source of life— God Himself. This dependence manifests in practices like daily prayer, Scripture reading, and seeking God's presence in all aspects of life. Just as Adam and Eve were invited to eat from the Tree of Life, believers today are invited to partake in the spiritual sustenance that God offers through a relationship with Him. In moments of weakness or spiritual dryness, the Tree of Life reminds us to return to the wellspring of life that is found in God's presence.

2. Nourishment Through Scripture and Prayer:

- Daily Bread for the Soul: Just as physical trees provide fruit for nourishment, the Tree of Life represents the spiritual sustenance we need to grow and flourish. One way believers can access this nourishment is through the Word of God. Scripture is often referred to as food for the soul (Matthew 4:4), and meditating on God's Word is a vital practice for spiritual growth. Additionally, prayer is a way to "eat" from the Tree of Life, as it deepens our relationship with God and allows us to draw closer to Him.

- Personal Reflection: How can I prioritize time with God to ensure I am being nourished spiritually? Reflecting on the Tree of Life can inspire a renewed commitment to spiritual disciplines. This might mean setting aside dedicated time for prayer, Scripture study, or quiet reflection each day. Like the tree that bears fruit continually in the new creation (Revelation 22:2), spiritual growth is an ongoing process that requires regular nourishment from God.

2. Embracing God's Wisdom for Life

1. Seeking Divine Wisdom:

- The Tree of Life as Wisdom: In the book of Proverbs, wisdom is described as a "tree of life" to those who take hold of it (Proverbs 3:18). This connection between wisdom and the Tree of Life suggests that spiritual growth involves not only drawing closer to God but also living in alignment with His wisdom. Embracing God's wisdom brings spiritual vitality, direction, and purpose.

- Personal Reflection: In what areas of my life do I need to seek God's wisdom more fully? Whether in relationships, decisions, or struggles, seeking wisdom from God is essential for personal spiritual growth. The Tree of Life invites us to be lifelong learners of God's truth, growing in understanding as we apply biblical principles to our everyday lives. By actively seeking wisdom—through prayer, studying Scripture, and seeking wise counsel—we position ourselves to experience the flourishing life that God intends.

2. Avoiding Spiritual Bypasses:

- Choosing Life Over False Wisdom: The Tree of Life contrasts with the Tree of the Knowledge of Good and Evil, which brought death and separation from God. This contrast highlights the importance of discerning between true wisdom, which leads to life, and false wisdom, which leads to spiritual death. Spiritual growth involves rejecting shortcuts, pride, and self-reliance in favor of humility and trust in God's ways.

- Personal Reflection: Am I pursuing true wisdom from God, or am I relying on my own understanding? Reflecting on the Tree of Life helps us identify areas where we might be tempted to rely on worldly wisdom or our own strength, rather than seeking God's guidance. The call to spiritual growth is a call to choose life—to seek the life-giving wisdom that comes from God rather than following paths that lead to emptiness or disconnection from Him.

3. Living in Hope of Eternal Life

1. Anticipating the Fulfillment of God's Promise:

- The Promise of Eternal Life: The Tree of Life is a symbol of eternal life, both in its original setting in Eden and in its restored form in the new Jerusalem (Revelation 22:2). For believers, spiritual growth involves living with the hope and assurance that eternal life is not just a future promise but also a present reality through faith in Christ. This hope shapes how we live, giving us the courage to persevere and the motivation to grow closer to God.

- Personal Reflection: How does my hope in eternal life influence my daily actions and decisions? Reflecting on the Tree of Life can help us keep an eternal perspective, reminding us that our spiritual growth has both present and eternal significance. When we live with the awareness of God's eternal promises, we are more likely to prioritize spiritual growth, knowing that our relationship with God will endure forever.

2. Persevering in Faith:

- Overcoming Through Christ: Revelation 2:7 promises that those who are victorious in their faith will be given the right to eat from the Tree of Life. This promise serves as an encouragement to persevere, even in the face of difficulties or spiritual challenges. Spiritual growth is not always easy, but the Tree of Life reminds us of the reward that awaits those who endure and remain faithful to God.

- Personal Reflection: Where do I need to strengthen my perseverance in faith? Reflecting on the Tree of Life can provide encouragement in seasons of struggle. Whether dealing with personal doubts, external trials, or spiritual fatigue, the Tree of Life serves as a reminder that perseverance leads to eternal life. When we hold on to God's promises and trust in His sustaining grace, we grow stronger in our faith and spiritual maturity.

4. Sharing Spiritual Nourishment with Others

1. Bearing Spiritual Fruit:

- Fruit for the World: The Tree of Life continually bears fruit, providing nourishment and healing for the nations (Revelation 22:2). This image invites believers to consider how their spiritual growth can extend beyond personal benefit to positively impact others. Just as the Tree of Life offers sustenance and healing, believers are called to bear spiritual fruit that blesses those around them.

- Personal Reflection: How can my spiritual growth benefit others? Reflecting on the Tree of Life challenges us to consider how we can be sources of life and encouragement for those around us. Spiritual growth should result in bearing fruit—acts of kindness, generosity, love, and service—that bring healing and hope to others. As we grow in our relationship with God, we become vessels of His life-giving presence to those in need of spiritual nourishment.

2. Promoting Healing and Reconciliation:

- Healing for the Nations: The Tree of Life's leaves are for the healing of the nations, symbolizing God's redemptive plan for the whole world. As followers of Christ, we are called to participate in this healing work by promoting reconciliation, justice, and peace in our communities and beyond. Spiritual growth involves developing a heart for healing—not only within ourselves but also in the brokenness we see in the world.

- Personal Reflection: In what ways can I be an agent of healing in my relationships or community? Reflecting on the Tree of Life encourages us to actively seek ways to bring healing to those around us. This might involve extending forgiveness, seeking reconciliation, or advocating for justice in areas of brokenness. As we grow spiritually, we are called to reflect the healing power of God's grace in our interactions with others.

The Tree of Life offers a rich symbol for personal spiritual growth, inviting believers to reflect on their relationship with God, their dependence on His wisdom, and their hope in eternal life. By drawing spiritual nourishment from God, embracing His wisdom, living in hope of eternal life, and sharing that life with others, believers can experience the fullness of the spiritual growth that God desires for them.

As we reflect on the Tree of Life, we are reminded that spiritual growth is an ongoing journey—one that requires regular sustenance, perseverance, and a heart open to God's transformative work. Through daily communion with God, seeking His wisdom, and living out the hope of eternal life, we are empowered to grow into the fullness of who God has created us to be.

of healing. Worship is a time when the congregation comes together to encounter God's presence, and it can be a space for emotional, spiritual, and even physical healing. As the church gathers to worship, the community collectively seeks the presence of God, who alone can provide the deep healing that the Tree of Life symbolizes. Through prayer, confession, and the proclamation of God's Word, worship becomes a healing balm for those who are wounded, tired, or broken.

- Reflection for Worship: How can our worship services foster healing in our community? Reflecting on the Tree of Life encourages churches to be intentional in creating spaces where people can come as they are and find healing through the presence of God. This might include times of prayer for the sick, opportunities for confession and reconciliation, or simply fostering a welcoming environment where people feel safe to express their hurts and seek God's restoration.

2. A Mission to Heal the Nations:

- Extending Healing Beyond the Church Walls: The healing leaves of the Tree of Life are not just for the church but for the nations, reflecting God's redemptive plan for the whole world. The church, as the body of Christ, is called to be a vessel of this healing in the broader community and world. This mission involves not only proclaiming the gospel but also actively working to bring healing to areas of brokenness in society, such as injustice, poverty, and relational strife.

- The Role of Worship in Empowering Mission: Worship plays a central role in preparing and empowering the church for its mission of healing. In worship, believers are reminded of God's heart for the nations and His desire to bring reconciliation and restoration to all people. Worship renews the church's vision for its role in the world, inspiring members to go out and be agents of healing in their communities. This can include participating in acts of justice, mercy, and outreach that reflect the healing power of the gospel.

- Reflection for Worship and Mission: How can our worship services inspire and equip the church for its mission of healing? Reflecting on the Tree of Life challenges churches to make the connection between worship and mission more explicit. Worship should not be an end in itself but a launching point for believers to go out and live out the gospel in tangible ways. This might involve focusing on themes of justice, mercy, and healing in sermons, prayers, and songs, as well as providing opportunities for congregants to engage in outreach and service.

3. The Tree of Life and Church Life

1. Spiritual Nourishment in Community:

- The Church as a Source of Spiritual Nourishment: Just as the Tree of Life provides continual fruit for sustenance, the church is called to be a place where believers are spiritually nourished. This nourishment comes through regular engagement with the Word of God, the sacraments, and the fellowship of believers. In church life, members are fed spiritually through worship, teaching, discipleship, and community, enabling them to grow in their faith and relationship with God.

- Reflection for Church Life: How can our church better provide spiritual nourishment for its members? Reflecting on the Tree of Life encourages church leaders to consider how they are cultivating environments that foster spiritual growth. This might include offering more opportunities for Bible study, small groups, and prayer gatherings, as well as ensuring that worship services are designed to lead people deeper into God's presence.

2. Bearing Fruit for the World:

- The Church as a Fruit-Bearing Community: The Tree of Life continuously bears fruit in the new creation, symbolizing the ongoing, life-giving nature of God's presence. Similarly, the church is called to be a fruit-bearing community, producing spiritual fruit that blesses others. The fruit of the Spirit—love, joy, peace, patience, kindness, goodness, faithfulness, gentleness, and self-control (Galatians 5:22-23)—should be evident in the life of the church, reflecting the transformative power of God's Spirit at work.

- Reflection for Church Life: How can our church cultivate a culture of bearing fruit for the world? Reflecting on the Tree of Life challenges churches to focus on both internal spiritual growth and outward expressions of that growth through service, outreach, and evangelism. Churches can consider how they are equipping members to live out their faith in the world, bearing fruit that reflects the love and character of Christ. This might involve creating more opportunities for service, fostering a culture of generosity, or encouraging members to engage with their local communities in meaningful ways.

4. The Tree of Life and Eternal Worship

1. Worship as a Foretaste of Eternity:

- Worship in Light of Eternity: The Tree of Life in Revelation 22 symbolizes the eternal life and healing that believers will experience in the new creation. In communal worship, the church experiences a foretaste of this eternal reality. Worship on earth is a reflection of the heavenly worship that will take place for eternity, where all nations will gather around the throne of God and the Lamb. The Tree of Life reminds the church that its worship is not just for the present moment but is a participation in the eternal worship that will one day be fully realized.

- Reflection for Worship: How can our worship reflect the hope of eternity? Reflecting on the Tree of Life invites the church to consider how its worship practices point toward the ultimate reality of eternal life with God. This might include incorporating themes of hope, resurrection, and the new creation into worship services, as well as emphasizing the joy and peace that come from knowing that believers will one day dwell in God's presence forever.

2. Living in Anticipation of the New Creation:

- The Church as a Sign of the Coming Kingdom: The Tree of Life's presence in the new Jerusalem points to the future fulfillment of God's redemptive plan. As the body of Christ, the church is called to live in anticipation of this coming kingdom, serving as a sign of God's future restoration in the present world. Through worship, service, and community life, the church embodies the hope of the new creation, showing the world a glimpse of the healing, peace, and life that will come when God's kingdom is fully realized.

- Reflection for Church Life: How can our church live more fully in anticipation of God's coming kingdom? Reflecting on the Tree of Life encourages churches to focus on being a foretaste of the kingdom in their worship and mission. This might include living out kingdom values such as justice, reconciliation, and peace, while maintaining a focus on the ultimate hope of resurrection and new creation. Churches can inspire their members to live in light of eternity, with the assurance that their worship and work on earth have eternal significance.

The Tree of Life is a powerful symbol that not only speaks to personal spiritual growth but also has profound implications for communal worship and church life. It calls the church to be a community that draws its life from God's presence, fosters healing and reconciliation, and bears fruit for the world. In worship, the church experiences a foretaste of the eternal life that the Tree of Life symbolizes, while in its communal life, the church reflects the unity, sustenance, and hope found in Christ.

As the church continues to gather in worship and live out its mission in the world, the Tree of Life serves as a reminder of the spiritual nourishment, healing, and eternal hope that come from being in relationship with God. By drawing on this rich biblical symbol, churches can deepen their worship practices, strengthen their communal life, and more fully embody the life-giving presence of God in the world.

Living Out the Symbol: Incorporating the Lessons of the Tree of Life into Daily Living

The Tree of Life, with its rich symbolism of eternal life, spiritual nourishment, and healing, is not only a theological concept but also a guide for daily Christian living. The lessons drawn from this powerful image can shape how believers live their lives, interact with others, and pursue a deeper relationship with God. Living out the symbol of the Tree of Life involves integrating its themes of dependence on God, growth through wisdom, and the call to be a source of healing and life for others.

In this chapter, we will explore practical ways to incorporate the lessons of the Tree of Life into daily living, focusing on personal faith, relationships, and the broader mission of being agents of life in the world.

1. Dependence on God for Spiritual Nourishment

1. Daily Communion with God:

- Seeking God's Sustenance: Just as the Tree of Life in Eden offered continual nourishment, believers are called to seek spiritual sustenance from God daily. This means maintaining a personal relationship with God through prayer, Scripture reading, and worship. Just as physical nourishment is necessary for health, spiritual nourishment is essential for growing in faith and living a life that reflects Christ's character.

- Practical Application: Begin each day by drawing near to God, asking for His guidance, strength, and wisdom. Set aside time for prayer and reflection, meditating on the truths of Scripture. Reflect on passages that emphasize God's provision and presence, such as Psalm 1:3, which compares a faithful person to a tree planted by streams of water, bearing fruit in season. Consider how to depend on God throughout the day, recognizing that He is the source of life and spiritual renewal.

2. Sustained Growth Through the Word:

- Nourishment Through Scripture: The Tree of Life offers a parallel to the Bible, which provides spiritual food for those seeking wisdom and growth. By immersing oneself in the Word of God, believers receive guidance and insight for daily living, leading to sustained spiritual growth.

- Practical Application: Develop a consistent habit of reading and meditating on Scripture. Choose a passage or book of the Bible to study deeply, asking God to reveal how its truths apply to your life. Reflect on passages like John 15:5, where Jesus describes Himself as the vine and believers as branches, emphasizing the importance of remaining connected to Him. Like the Tree of Life, God's Word is meant to be a continuous source of nourishment and wisdom.

2. Growth Through Wisdom and Righteousness

1. Pursuing Godly Wisdom:

- Wisdom as a Tree of Life: Proverbs 3:18 describes wisdom as a "tree of life to those who take hold of her." This verse teaches that godly wisdom is life-giving and essential for navigating life's challenges. Spiritual growth involves seeking wisdom from God and applying it to daily decisions, relationships, and responsibilities.

- Practical Application: Seek to cultivate godly wisdom by making prayer and discernment key parts of decision-making. Before making significant choices, take time to reflect, pray, and seek counsel from Scripture or other believers. Ask yourself: "Am I making this decision based on God's wisdom, or on my own understanding?" When faced with conflict or uncertainty, turn to the wisdom literature in the Bible (Proverbs, Ecclesiastes, James) for insights on how to act with righteousness, integrity, and discernment.

2. Living a Life of Righteousness:

- Bearing the Fruit of Righteousness: Proverbs 11:30 states, "The fruit of the righteous is a tree of life." Living a righteous life involves aligning actions, thoughts, and intentions with God's will. When believers live out righteousness, they bear spiritual fruit that blesses others and reflects the life-giving nature of the Tree of Life.

- Practical Application: Reflect on how your daily actions align with the principles of righteousness and integrity. Consider areas where you can grow in kindness, patience, humility, and service. Make a conscious effort to live in a way that reflects the character of Christ, allowing your life to be a witness to those around you. Small daily acts of righteousness—like offering a word of encouragement, practicing honesty in difficult situations, or choosing forgiveness over resentment—are ways to live out the lessons of the Tree of Life.

3. Becoming a Source of Healing and Life for Others

1. Extending Grace and Healing:

- Healing for the Nations: Revelation 22:2 describes the leaves of the Tree of Life as being "for the healing of the nations." This speaks to the church's calling to be a source of healing and reconciliation in a broken world. As individual members of the body of Christ, believers are called to bring healing into their relationships, communities, and workplaces.

- Practical Application: Be mindful of the role you can play in bringing healing to those around you. This might mean offering forgiveness to someone who has wronged you, helping to resolve conflicts, or supporting a friend or family member going through a difficult time. Look for opportunities to be a source of peace and restoration, whether through kind words, acts of service, or simply listening with empathy. Consider how your presence in different settings can bring the life-giving power of Christ to others.

2. Sharing the Life of Christ:

- Bearing Fruit That Impacts Others: Just as the Tree of Life bears fruit that provides nourishment, believers are called to bear spiritual fruit that blesses others. The fruit of the Spirit—love, joy, peace, patience, kindness, goodness, faithfulness, gentleness, and self-control (Galatians 5:22-23)—should be evident in the way believers interact with others.

- Practical Application: Look for ways to share the fruit of the Spirit in your daily interactions. Be intentional about expressing kindness, patience, and love in your relationships, both at home and in the wider community. Think about specific ways you can serve those in need, whether through volunteering, mentoring, or simply being a source of encouragement to those around you. Living out the lessons of the Tree of Life means actively seeking to bless others and bring the life of Christ into the world through your actions.

4. Living in Hope of Eternal Life

1. Keeping an Eternal Perspective:

- The Promise of Eternal Life: The Tree of Life is a symbol of eternal life, reminding believers of the future hope they have in Christ. This eternal perspective can shape how we live each day, helping us prioritize what matters most and live with purpose.

- Practical Application: Cultivate an eternal perspective by reflecting on the promises of Scripture regarding eternal life. In moments of difficulty or stress, remind yourself that the trials of this world are temporary and that your ultimate hope is in the life to come. Consider how the hope of eternity can help you live with greater courage, generosity, and purpose. Let this perspective shape how you use your time, talents, and resources, focusing on what has lasting value in God's kingdom.

2. Persevering Through Challenges:

- Perseverance in Faith: Revelation 2:7 promises that those who overcome will be given the right to eat from the Tree of Life. This promise encourages believers to persevere in their faith, even in the face of trials. The hope of eternal life provides strength and motivation to keep pressing forward.

- Practical Application: When facing challenges, remind yourself of the promise of eternal life and the reward of remaining faithful to God. Pray for endurance and strength, trusting that God will sustain you through difficult seasons. Surround yourself with a community of believers who can encourage and support you, and find comfort in the knowledge that God's promises are sure. Let the hope of the Tree of Life inspire you to persevere with faith and hope, knowing that eternal life awaits those who remain faithful.

Living out the lessons of the Tree of Life involves integrating its themes of spiritual nourishment, growth through wisdom, healing, and eternal hope into daily life. As believers seek God's presence, pursue righteousness, and extend healing to others, they reflect the life-giving power of the Tree of Life in their everyday actions. The promise of eternal life offers hope and motivation, encouraging believers to live with purpose and perseverance, trusting in God's plan for their lives.

The Tree of Life is more than just a theological concept; it is a model for how believers are called to live. By drawing near to God for spiritual sustenance, seeking His wisdom, bearing fruit that blesses others, and living in the hope of eternity, believers can embody the life and healing that the Tree of Life represents.

CONCLUSION

Recap of the Tree of Life's Journey Through Scripture

The Tree of Life serves as a profound and powerful symbol that weaves throughout the biblical narrative, from Genesis to Revelation. Its journey through Scripture reveals key themes of God's provision, eternal life, wisdom, healing, and restoration, all of which reflect God's redemptive plan for humanity and creation.

1. The Tree of Life in the Garden of Eden

The first appearance of the Tree of Life occurs in the Garden of Eden (Genesis 2:9), where it represents God's desire for humanity to live in eternal communion with Him. Adam and Eve had access to this tree, a symbol of divine provision and the abundant life God intended for them. However, after the fall, they were barred from the Tree of Life, signifying the separation from God that sin brings. The loss of access to the Tree of Life sets the stage for the unfolding narrative of redemption throughout Scripture, where God seeks to restore what was lost.

2. The Tree of Life in Wisdom Literature

In the wisdom literature, particularly in Proverbs, the Tree of Life becomes a metaphor for living in alignment with God's wisdom. Proverbs 3:18 describes wisdom as "a tree of life to those who take hold of her," highlighting the connection between divine wisdom and flourishing life. This shift in symbolism emphasizes that spiritual vitality and growth come through embracing God's wisdom and living righteously. The Tree of Life here represents not only the hope of eternal life but the daily nourishment and direction that come from living wisely.

3. The Tree of Life and Redemption Through Christ

Theologically, the Tree of Life points forward to Christ's redemptive work. In the New Testament, the cross of Christ is often described as a "tree" (Acts 5:30, Galatians 3:13), symbolizing the path back to eternal life. Through His death and resurrection, Jesus restores what was lost in the fall, providing believers with access to eternal life once again. The cross, as the tree of redemption, becomes the means by which believers can partake in the eternal life symbolized by the Tree of Life.

4. The Tree of Life in the New Jerusalem

The final and climactic appearance of the Tree of Life is found in Revelation 22, where it stands in the New Jerusalem, offering healing to the nations and bearing fruit continually. This vision represents the full restoration of God's creation, where sin, death, and suffering are no more. The Tree of Life, which was once lost due to sin, is now fully accessible, symbolizing the eternal life and communion with God that believers will enjoy in the new creation. It is not just a return to Eden but a fulfillment of God's ultimate plan of redemption and restoration for all creation.

5. The Practical Implications of the Tree of Life

The lessons of the Tree of Life extend beyond theological reflection and serve as a guide for personal spiritual growth and community life. As a symbol of spiritual nourishment, wisdom, and healing, the Tree of Life calls believers to depend on God for sustenance, pursue godly wisdom in their daily lives, and be sources of healing and life for others. The hope of eternal life, represented by the Tree of Life, encourages believers to persevere in faith and live with an eternal perspective, knowing that their present actions have lasting significance in God's redemptive plan.

Conclusion: The Tree of Life as a Symbol of God's Redemptive Plan

The journey of the Tree of Life through Scripture reflects the entirety of God's redemptive story—His original design for humanity, the tragic consequences of sin, and the ultimate hope of restoration through Christ. It is a symbol that calls believers to live in daily dependence on God, to seek wisdom and righteousness, and to embody the healing and life that Christ offers.

As believers anticipate the full restoration of creation, the Tree of Life stands as a beacon of hope, reminding us that God's plan is not just to restore what was lost but to fulfill His promises of eternal life and communion with Him. Through the lessons of the Tree of Life, we are called to live lives that reflect the eternal, life-giving presence of God, both now and for eternity.

FINAL THOUGHTS

THE ENDURING SIGNIFICANCE OF THE TREET OF LIFE IN CHRISTIN FAITH AND PRACTICE

Final Thoughts: The Enduring Significance of the Tree of Life in Christian Faith and Practice

The Tree of Life is one of the most enduring and powerful symbols in the Bible, representing themes that are central to the Christian faith—eternal life, divine provision, wisdom, healing, and restoration. Its presence from the beginning of Scripture to its final appearance in Revelation reveals the depth of God's redemptive plan for humanity, offering both a timeless reminder of His faithfulness and a forward-looking hope for what is to come.

1. A Symbol of God's Eternal Provision

At its core, the Tree of Life reflects God's desire to provide life, both physically and spiritually, for His creation. From the Garden of Eden, where it symbolized the perfect life God intended for humanity, to the New Jerusalem, where it signifies the fulfillment of God's redemptive plan, the Tree of Life reminds us that God is the ultimate source of life. As believers, we are continually invited to draw near to God, the giver of life, and depend on His provision for our spiritual nourishment and growth.

In Christian practice, this calls us to live in daily communion with God, seeking His presence through prayer, worship, and Scripture. Just as the Tree of Life provided sustenance to Adam and Eve, we are sustained by our relationship with God, finding strength, wisdom, and grace in Him. The Tree of Life serves as a powerful reminder that our ultimate life source is found in God alone.

2. The Pursuit of Wisdom and Righteousness

The Tree of Life's connection to wisdom, particularly in the book of Proverbs, highlights the importance of living a life aligned with God's truth. Wisdom, described as "a tree of life to those who take hold of her" (Proverbs 3:18), is essential for spiritual growth and flourishing. In Christian practice, this emphasizes the need for believers to seek God's wisdom in all areas of life, making decisions that reflect His righteousness and truth.

Incorporating the lessons of the Tree of Life means striving to live wisely, in accordance with God's will, and pursuing a life of integrity, justice, and compassion. The pursuit of wisdom is not just an intellectual exercise; it is a way of life that leads to spiritual vitality and a deeper connection with God. The Tree of Life reminds us that as we seek and apply godly wisdom, we experience the abundant life that God intends for us.

3. A Call to Be Agents of Healing and Reconciliation

The image of the Tree of Life in Revelation 22, with its leaves for the healing of the nations, calls Christians to be agents of healing and reconciliation in a broken world. As followers of Christ, we are invited to participate in God's redemptive work by bringing healing to the people and places around us. This may involve acts of kindness, compassion, forgiveness, and justice—offering hope and restoration to those in need.

In Christian practice, this calls the church to embody the healing power of the gospel in tangible ways. Whether through acts of service, community building, or advocating for peace and justice, the church is called to reflect the life-giving presence of God in the world. The Tree of Life challenges us to go beyond personal spiritual growth and extend the love, grace, and healing of Christ to others, both within and outside the church.

4. A Symbol of Hope for Eternal Life

The final vision of the Tree of Life in the New Jerusalem represents the culmination of God's promise of eternal life. For Christians, this offers hope not only for the future but for the present as well. The Tree of Life serves as a reminder that eternal life begins now, through a relationship with Christ, and continues into the age to come when all things will be restored. This hope shapes how we live today, encouraging us to persevere in faith and live with purpose, knowing that God's promises will one day be fully realized.

In Christian faith and practice, the hope of eternal life provides comfort in times of trial and motivation to live a life that honors God. The Tree of Life invites believers to live with an eternal perspective, prioritizing what matters most—our relationship with God, the love we show to others, and the pursuit of righteousness. As we look forward to the day when we will eat from the Tree of Life in God's eternal kingdom, we are called to live lives that reflect the reality of God's kingdom here and now.

Enduring Significance in Christian Life

The Tree of Life remains a timeless symbol of God's presence, faithfulness, and the hope of eternal life. Its journey through Scripture serves as a reminder that, despite humanity's fall into sin, God's plan has always been to restore us to eternal communion with Him. In daily Christian practice, the Tree of Life inspires believers to seek spiritual nourishment, live wisely, pursue healing and reconciliation, and hold fast to the hope of eternal life.

As we live out these truths, the Tree of Life becomes more than a symbol; it becomes a way of life that reflects the abundant, eternal life that God offers through Jesus Christ. This life, both now and in eternity, is the ultimate gift of God's grace, and the Tree of Life stands as a powerful testament to His redemptive love and unending faithfulness.

The Tree of Life reminds us that the story of redemption is ongoing, and as we await its ultimate fulfillment, we are invited to live each day in the light of God's promises, drawing from His life-giving presence and sharing that life with the world.

APPENDICES

BIBLICAL REFERENCES

Comprehensive List of All Scripture References Discussed

This appendix provides a comprehensive list of all the biblical references cited in the discussion of the Tree of Life, its symbolism, and its significance throughout Scripture. These passages explore the Tree of Life from its initial appearance in Genesis to its fulfillment in Revelation, along with other significant biblical themes related to life, wisdom, healing, and redemption.

1. The Tree of Life in the Garden of Eden

- Genesis 2:9 – The Tree of Life and the Tree of the Knowledge of Good and Evil in the Garden of Eden.

- Genesis 3:22-24 — Humanity's expulsion from the Garden and loss of access to the Tree of Life after the fall.

2. The Tree of Life in Wisdom Literature

- Proverbs 3:18 — Wisdom is described as a tree of life to those who take hold of her.

- Proverbs 11:30 — The fruit of the righteous is a tree of life.

- Proverbs 13:12 — Hope deferred makes the heart sick, but a desire fulfilled is a tree of life.

- Proverbs 15:4 — A soothing tongue is a tree of life, but a perverse tongue crushes the spirit.

3. The Tree of Life and Redemption Through Christ

- Acts 5:30 — The cross of Christ is described as a "tree" upon which He was hung.

- Galatians 3:13 — Christ redeemed us from the curse of the law by becoming a curse for us, for it is written: "Cursed is everyone who is hung on a tree."

- 1 Peter 2:24 — Christ bore our sins in His body on the tree, so that we might die to sins and live for righteousness.

4. The Tree of Life in the New Jerusalem

- Revelation 2:7 – The promise to the one who overcomes: access to the Tree of Life in the paradise of God.

- Revelation 22:1-2 – The Tree of Life in the New Jerusalem, on either side of the river of the water of life, bearing fruit each month, and its leaves are for the healing of the nations.

- Revelation 22:14 – Blessed are those who wash their robes, that they may have the right to the Tree of Life and may enter the city through the gates.

- Revelation 22:19 – A warning that anyone who takes away from the words of prophecy will be denied access to the Tree of Life.

5. Related Biblical Themes and Symbols

- Genesis 3:7 – Adam and Eve's use of fig leaves to cover themselves after their disobedience.

- Psalm 1:3 – The righteous person is like a tree planted by streams of water, yielding fruit in season.

- John 15:5 – Jesus describes Himself as the vine, and believers as branches who must remain in Him to bear fruit.

- John 10:28 – Jesus promises eternal life to those who follow Him.

- John 6:35 – Jesus declares, "I am the bread of life. Whoever comes to me will never go hungry, and whoever believes in me will never be thirsty."

- Romans 11:17-24 – Paul's metaphor of the olive tree and the grafting of Gentile believers into the people of God.

- Galatians 5:22-23 – The fruit of the Spirit: love, joy, peace, patience, kindness, goodness, faithfulness, gentleness, and self-control.

- Isaiah 53:5 – "By His wounds we are healed," reflecting Christ's role in spiritual healing and restoration.

- Revelation 21:4 – A vision of the new creation, where there will be no more death, mourning, crying, or pain.

6. The Role of Trees in the Ancient Near East and Biblical Metaphor

- Genesis 8:11 – The dove returns to Noah with an olive leaf, symbolizing the end of God's judgment and the restoration of life.

- Matthew 21:18-19 – Jesus curses the barren fig tree as a symbol of judgment against fruitlessness.

- John 3:5-6 – Jesus teaches about being born of water and the Spirit, reflecting spiritual rebirth and life in Him.

These biblical references provide a foundation for understanding the profound symbolism of the Tree of Life and its enduring significance in the Christian faith. From its early depiction in the Garden of Eden to its ultimate fulfillment in the New Jerusalem, the Tree of Life serves as a powerful image of God's provision, wisdom, healing, and eternal life. These passages invite believers to reflect on the role of the Tree of Life in their spiritual journey, reminding them of God's redemptive plan and their call to live in dependence on Him, pursue righteousness, and share the life-giving presence of Christ with the world.

GLOSSARY

DEFINITIONS OF KEY TERMS AND CONCEPTS

Further Reading: Recommended Books and Articles for Deeper Study

For those interested in delving deeper into the biblical, theological, and symbolic themes of the Tree of Life and related concepts, the following books and articles offer valuable insights. These resources cover topics such as biblical theology, wisdom literature, the significance of trees in the Bible, and eschatological themes like the new creation and eternal life.

1. Biblical Theology and the Tree of Life

- "Biblical Theology: Old and New Testaments" by Geerhardus Vos

- This classic work in biblical theology traces the overarching narrative of Scripture, including themes of creation, fall, redemption, and restoration. Vos' exploration of God's redemptive plan sheds light on the significance of the Tree of Life within the biblical story.

- "The Mission of God: Unlocking the Bible's Grand Narrative" by Christopher J.H. Wright

- Wright emphasizes the missional framework of the Bible and discusses how the themes of creation and restoration fit into God's ultimate plan for humanity. The book includes discussions on the Tree of Life and its role in the narrative arc of Scripture.

- "From Eden to the New Jerusalem: Exploring God's Plan for Life on Earth" by T. Desmond Alexander

- This book offers a comprehensive look at the biblical narrative from Eden to the new creation, with special focus on themes like the Tree of Life, divine presence, and eternal life. Alexander's work is a helpful resource for understanding how the biblical story unfolds through the symbolism of trees and life.

2. Wisdom Literature and the Tree of Life

- "Proverbs: Wisdom that Works" by Raymond C. Ortlund Jr.

- Ortlund's commentary on Proverbs explores the practical application of biblical wisdom and its connection to life. His analysis of the Tree of Life imagery in Proverbs 3:18 and 11:30 provides insights into the role of wisdom in spiritual growth and flourishing.

- "The Book of Proverbs: A Commentary" by Bruce K. Waltke

- Waltke's scholarly commentary offers an in-depth examination of the wisdom literature, focusing on the themes of life and wisdom in Proverbs. His work provides a detailed analysis of the metaphors and symbols, including the Tree of Life, in relation to living a righteous life.

- "The Tree of Life: Biblical Wisdom and Spiritual Growth" by Roland E. Murphy

- This work focuses specifically on the connection between wisdom and the Tree of Life in Scripture, offering insights into how biblical wisdom can lead to personal spiritual growth. Murphy provides a thoughtful exploration of how the Tree of Life serves as a symbol of God's life-giving wisdom.

3. Eschatology and Eternal Life

- "The Bible and the Future" by Anthony A. Hoekema

- Hoekema's comprehensive study of eschatology covers key themes like the resurrection, new creation, and eternal life. His discussion of the Tree of Life in the context of Revelation provides valuable insights into the significance of the tree in the new Jerusalem.

- "Heaven: The Ultimate Home" by Randy Alcorn

- Alcorn explores biblical descriptions of heaven and eternal life, offering practical reflections on the future hope that believers have in Christ. His discussion of the Tree of Life as a symbol of eternal life in the new creation is both theological and pastoral, helping readers to understand its relevance for daily living.

- "A New Heaven and a New Earth: Reclaiming Biblical Eschatology" by J. Richard Middleton

- Middleton provides a robust biblical theology of the new creation, focusing on God's plan to restore all things. His discussion of the Tree of Life as part of the new Jerusalem is rooted in a biblical understanding of renewal and redemption.

4. The Symbolism of Trees and Creation in the Bible

- "The Meaning of Trees: Botany, History, Healing, and Lore" by Fred Hageneder

- Though not specifically focused on the Bible, this book provides a fascinating look at the symbolism of trees throughout history and various cultures, including the biblical context. It explores the spiritual and healing qualities attributed to trees, making it a helpful resource for understanding the broader cultural significance of trees, including the Tree of Life.

- "The Bible and Ecology: Rediscovering the Community of Creation" by Richard Bauckham

- Bauckham explores the relationship between humanity, creation, and God, focusing on ecological themes within Scripture. His work offers insights into the role of trees, including the Tree of Life, within the broader context of creation care and the restoration of the natural world.

- "The Glory of the Tree: An Illustrated History" by Noel Kingsbury

- This beautifully illustrated book explores the history and symbolism of trees in religious and cultural contexts, including the biblical narrative. Kingsbury touches on the theological significance of trees in Scripture, providing readers with a visual and historical appreciation for the Tree of Life and its counterparts.

5. Articles and Journals for Further Study

- "The Tree of Life: A Theological and Symbolic Study" by Gordon J. Wenham, Journal for the Study of the Old Testament

- Wenham's article explores the symbolism and theological implications of the Tree of Life, particularly in the context of Genesis and Revelation. This academic study provides an in-depth analysis of how the Tree of Life functions within the biblical narrative.

- "The Tree of Life in Biblical Theology" by Tremper Longman III, Themelios

- Longman examines the role of the Tree of Life as a symbol of divine provision and eternal life, tracing its significance across the canon of Scripture. This journal article is a useful resource for readers interested in the theological implications of the Tree of Life.

- "The Tree of Life in Proverbs: A Study of Biblical Imagery" by Katharine J. Dell, Vetus Testamentum

- Dell's article focuses on the Tree of Life in the wisdom literature, particularly in the book of Proverbs. It offers insights into the metaphorical use of the Tree of Life and its relationship to wisdom, righteousness, and spiritual growth.

6. Christian Spirituality and Practical Application

- "Sacred Rhythms: Arranging Our Lives for Spiritual Transformation" by Ruth Haley Barton

- Barton's work offers practical insights into spiritual disciplines and how they can help believers experience deeper communion with God. This book emphasizes themes of spiritual nourishment and growth, reflecting the life-giving power of the Tree of Life in everyday spiritual practice.

- "The Celebration of Discipline: The Path to Spiritual Growth" by Richard Foster

- Foster's classic work on the spiritual disciplines provides practical guidance for living a life of spiritual vitality. The themes of nourishment, growth, and perseverance are all key to Foster's approach, mirroring the lessons of the Tree of Life in Christian practice.

- "Life Together: The Classic Exploration of Christian Community" by Dietrich Bonhoeffer

- Bonhoeffer's exploration of Christian community emphasizes the importance of mutual support, healing, and spiritual growth within the body of Christ. This book offers a framework for understanding how the church can reflect the life-giving and healing nature of the Tree of Life.

These recommended books and articles provide a variety of perspectives on the biblical, theological, and symbolic significance of the Tree of Life. Whether you are interested in deepening your understanding of biblical theology, exploring the practical applications of Christian spirituality, or studying the broader symbolism of trees in Scripture, these resources offer valuable insights for further reflection and study. By engaging with these works, readers can gain a richer appreciation of the enduring significance of the Tree of Life in the Christian faith.